Managing Global Logistics for Business Growth

A guide for small to medium enterprises pursuing the global markets through cross border trade (export/import).

Authored by Anthony "Tony" Barone

Published by Buoyant Capital, NYC, USA

Produced by Ray Garcia

Copyright 2016 all worldwide rights reserved

ISBN-13:978-1523448890
ISBN-10:152344889X
BISAC: Business & Economics / Exports & Imports

For bulk orders contact Ray Garcia at ray@bcap.biz

Preface

By some estimates the global economy consists of 7 billion people and 100 trillion dollars of purchasing power. By any measure - wherever the business is located- most of the world's commerce is outside its national boundaries. Unless the business is a laundromat or ice cream shop, it is going to be buying and selling in the global market if the business is to survive. That means having management with a grasp of the mechanics of global business. There are many books about the marketing, legal and financial aspects of international trade. This book is about practical issues of shipping, customs and getting paid. It seeks to address the problem of "not knowing what you do not know" even if there is a lot you already know.

About the Author

Anthony (Tony) Barone's thirty-five year international business career is entirely in global cross border trade. He has held vice president and director level positions in the manufacturing and logistics services sectors at both large and small companies including Pfizer and UTI. From 1988 to 2003 he was managing director of the Hanover Group specializing in international logistics and systems. He has served as an advisor to the World Customs Organization (2006-2014); the U.S. Department of Commerce Supply Chain Competitiveness Committee (2012-2014) and the Departmental Advisory Committee on the Commercial Operations of U.S. Customs (2006 - 2009). As Chair of Customs and Trade Facilitation at the International Chamber Of Commerce (2011- 2014) he helped identify the common cross border trade problems of small to medium enterprises expanding into the global market. He was an adjunct professor of Supply Chain Management at Rutgers University (2011 - 2015) and taught professional education courses at New York's World Trade Institute from 1988 to 1993. In 1995, Tony co-authored the college textbook "International Logistics" published by Springer Science+Business Media. Tony is a graduate of Columbia University and received a Masters of Business Administration in general management from Fairleigh Dickinson University. His work in global supply chain facilitation continues with advisory consulting for SMEs to address the problems faced by traders at borders around the world.

What is this book about?

This book is comprised of six parts deal treating interrelated topics – Bumps in the Road, Shipping and Regulatory Issues, Paying and Getting Paid and Expanding Into a Global Network. The book concludes with results from a survey highlighting the logistics barriers companies have experienced, and a compendium of common trade terms.

Bumps In The Road - It is informative to read what small and medium enterprises (SMEs) active in global business have to say about the difficulties they encounter every day. The book starts with the five most common problems companies experience and the underlying cause of those problems.

Transportation ("shipping") - Competitiveness in the global marketplace is inextricably linked to shipping. This section covers shipping costs, how to exploit transportation opportunities, protecting against physical loss, working with service providers and border security regimes that cause unpredictable delays.

Regulatory - If anything can be said about international trade it is that no matter what country the business is in, merchandise trade is regulated and those regulations are difficult but necessary to deal with. This section discusses customs and other border management issues.

Financing Trade - The getting paid section is about collecting payment for goods and paying for goods sourced with a special emphasis on bank systems of guarantee. This section covers a variety of topics related to the management of multiple foreign operations, global sourcing, sales and operations planning, automation and working expert resources.

Expanding into a global network is about those supply chain management problems that arise from increased transaction volume and multiple sites. Elements of the previous topics are introduced as relevant to building an integrated network.

The book concludes with a dictionary of trade terms and compendia of responses to the "bumps in the road" survey.

Table of Contents

Part I - Introduction

There are a lot of reasons why companies go global. A particular foreign market may present a greater profitability opportunity than the local market of the business. Perhaps, the business has reached the tipping point in its export business and the market has grown large enough to merit an additional manufacturing facility or partner in another country. Maybe access to skilled, lower-cost workers is an attraction. Possibly setting up a local shop in a foreign market will help circumvent trade barriers that are constraining the company's growth.

The rationale for expanding globally could be a personal lifestyle choice of spending the spring in Tuscany or the holiday season in Bavaria. I knew a fellow whose sole reason for starting a (successful) trading business in rugs was so he could travel the world.

Whatever the reason, growing merchandise-based companies that go global are sooner or later forced to face a myriad of new challenges. This book is about the logistics challenges of getting goods from place to place, across borders, economically, without running afoul of the folks who guard the world's borders.

Setting expectations is important, this book is a "reader," not a reference book. It is meant to be read, feet up, wine glass or beer beside you, in one or two sittings. You may find the hyperlinks helpful and bookmark a page or two for further study. But this is not a tome that you will keep on your desk for reference as you might keep Gray's Anatomy. Instead, the goal is that you learn things immediately useful about the logistical processes involved going global.

The secondary goal is to expose those potential pitfall topics that you may not have considered—to quote Donald Rumsfeld, "we do not know what we do not know." Hopefully, by the time you have finished this book, you will have identified some of those previously unknown issues and learned enough to seek expert help, whether that is with regard to customs, insurance, banking, or shipping.

The book is for small to medium enterprises (SME), a business that has grown beyond the "start-up venture". The SME would be an ongoing business, with employees, receivables, and payables. It has a business growth plan, and as the manager you know what business you are in and have the resources to expand. SMEs typically do not have a cadre of specialists, particularly where logistics and trade compliance are concerned. Those duties are most likely being added to existing staff with similar domestic responsibilities. However, realize that global is not the same as local business, it is outside of common knowledge and there are matters that managers need to understand better so they do not make serious mistakes in the process of going global.

There is another fact of managing an SME, they are not a multi-billion-dollar, multi-national enterprise (MNE) with lots of resources to allocate to every problem. I have worked for and consulted to, big MNEs and SMEs, and I have sold and bought services for both. The big MNE has tremendous advantages in purchasing leverage, expert resources, and brand credibility. That is what SMEs are competing against and therefore need to avoid making costly mistakes. SMEs must be quick, nimble, have insight into opportunities, and act deliberately, when they find opportunities. These are skills that can be learned and need to be mastered.

In some ways, there are advantages to being an SME. Multi-nationals are so large that they cannot change fast. Like great elephants or big aircraft carriers their mere size prevent them from responding quickly to changed market conditions. Internal bureaucracies slow them down. As an SME manager you can use nimbleness to spot and exploit opportunities in your target industry as they arise. The world is a huge place. While MNEs are spread all over, it is impossible for them to be first in class everywhere. I remember a former executive of General Motors, before the fall, saying "all big companies are small companies somewhere!" Those are weak spots that the SME can exploit with adroitness as those outliers wait for "home office" approval and guidance.

Not all SMEs enter the global marketplace on their own. Many, I would say most, go global as suppliers of bigger companies. After all, there are millions of companies worldwide, but fewer than 500 make up 70% of world trade! (http://www.gatt.org/trastat_e.html).

The majority of SMEs are supplying multi-national companies that are buying for manufacturing inputs for one or many manufacturing sites. Nissan is not just located in the United States and Japan. Neither is Nestle nor Pfizer nor

AGIP. There is an advantage to large companies signing multi-site supply contracts and for volume incentive to supplying them. That makes the SME supplying big multi-nationals in many different markets a global exporter and that requires expertise beyond shipping within the local market.

SMEs that export to MNEs at foreign locations are what fuels growth. As demand grows, the need to expand with owned factories or contract manufacturing arrangements grows and the SMEs are faced with their own need to locate new suppliers who are better suited economically or strategically to facilitate long-term, multi-location sustainability. With that comes more challenges and more unknowns. The SME starts to mature into a global entity and that means adopting globalization processes. There is an increasing need to understand customs issues, regulatory matters in foreign lands, shipping costs that the SME can sustain, and assuring that it gets paid in transactions between countries outside of its own.

There is a saying attributed to General George Marshall—"Strategy is for amateurs, logistics is for professionals!" To succeed in global business, companies need to manage both the cost and service aspects of global shipping and to avoid the regulatory traps and unpredictability that can delay shipments indefinitely. This is true both of exporters supplying international customers and importers buying from international vendors for internal use or resale.

In the next section we highlight the problems of moving goods cross border with the term "bumps in the road"!

Border Bumps and Barriers

When I was chair of the Customs and Trade Facilitation Commission of the International Chamber of Commerce in Paris, I conducted a survey of trade barriers. There were 350 respondents from 34 countries across 19 industrial sectors ranging from agriculture to transportation equipment. That is not a large sampling considering that there are over 300,000 exporters from the United States alone.

http://www.trade.gov/mas/ian/build/groups/public/@tg_ian/documents/webcontent/tg_ian_005410.pdf

Even with a limited sample size the consistency of problems across industries and geographies suggests that these issues are common.

The top five barriers to doing business globally were reported as:

1. Duty

2. VAT assessments

3. Classification uncertainty

4. Valuation issues

5. Unnecessary physical examinations

We will examine the first two in more depth.

Value of Goods in the Trade World

What is something worth? Well, one definition is "a good is worth what an unrelated person actually pays for it." What that unrelated person actually pays is the commercial value that must be declared on invoices presented at borders. This simple idea can get very confusing and cause a great deal of angst for reasons we will discuss in greater depth later. For now suffice to say customs authorities are naturally suspect that the value declared in commercial transactions is not the value that is ultimately actually paid or payable.

Duty & Value Added Tax

Duty is a tax on imports. While that is simple enough to say, figuring the official amount that is the basis for assessment is not so straight forward for a variety of reasons, one of which is mentioned above – suspicion that the value may not be the ultimate amount paid.

Similarly, VAT or "value added tax" which is generally a simple percentage calculation and payable by the importer in countries that use the VAT method of taxation, may be a bit more complicated to determine if the value itself is in question. Here again, simplicity turns complex. The fact that the regulations regarding VAT are different from country to country complicates matters further.

VAT is generally payable or guaranteed on entry of goods into a country. The tax is passed on when the goods are resold in the country of import. If the goods are re-exported, or used in manufacturing, the tax can be recovered on sale of the manufactured good. Duty can generally be recovered if the business or its client import an article and subsequently export it in the same form or make something with it that is subsequently exported. There are a variety of ways to accomplish the recovery of duty and taxes on imports. We will discuss these further below. The important thing here is to note that religiously recording value is important to both avoiding border delays <u>and</u> recovering monies later.

The primary document evidencing value is the commercial invoice. The commercial invoice is as much about customs as it is about billing the customer. Since unscrupulous traders commonly try to avoid duties, customs authorities are particularly interested in what it says.

For example, if the parties to a transaction are related, the value has to be the same *as if the parties were* unrelated. Customs value cannot be the "special" discounted price given when the goods are sold to a friend. If the business needs to discount the price legitimately and cannot prove it is an arm's-length price in a transaction, there is going to be a problem.

Transactions between related parties are a common problem area, especially since 70% of trade is between related entities. However, the world was not always that way. Systems of valuation for customs originated at a time when the buyer and seller were mostly not the same person. To accommodate evolving world trade a body of practice has arisen that defines how pricing between related parties should be developed, for customs and taxation purposes. These "conventions" are for governmental purposes. Internally, the business may have different transfer pricing policies for management purposes. Commercial invoices used for export and import must comply with internationally established rules. More on this later.

There are other supply chain interruptions that arise at borders related to value - particularly the deliberate under-declaration of transaction value in order to reduce or avoid duties and taxes, in other words, fraud. One method customs uses to spot fraud is comparing invoice values to similar transactions between other traders and even the same trader over time. Another way is to use reference pricing. For example, some countries have been known to use the automobile "Blue Book" to establish value.

There is another kind of valuation problem that arises out of legitimate business arrangements and the desire to properly report value. For example, the importer provides the seller with parts, or engineering expertise, to build a machine that will be imported at a subsequent time. The selling price on the transaction invoice does not show the value of the engineering investment. Value, in addition to that declared on an invoice, is called an "assist" and it needs to be taken into account. In this case, the true value of the machine includes the manufacturer's cost to build it, a profit, and the assist.

Another problem arises when an importer must pay the exporter a royalty at some subsequent time after the importation. For example, if the royalty is based on total sales in the importing country after goods are sold the royalty amount will not be known at the time of import and cannot be shown on the invoice at the time of import, this is because the royalty is paid later.

When additional payments are made subsequent to an importation, it is necessary to adjust the declared value at some later time or at the end of some accounting or fiscal period. Some countries do not allow this "reconciliation". Others do all reconciliation but there are a variety of methods of accomplishing this in the different countries.

The point is that issues related to both legitimate and fraudulent business practices are contributors to the problems that unpredictably hold up shipments.

Customs Classification Uncertainty

Concepts of value are not the only problems at borders that can hold up shipments. Classification is another issue directly related to the assessment of duty. Classification is the nomenclature of customs. The dictionary of goods used to assess duties and determine admissibility. The instrument containing this dictionary and the rate of duty applicable to each classification is the customs tariff.

Is a "peach" in a tin can a "fruit" or a "canned fruit" or is it a "foodstuff" or "dried fruit?" It might be all of these; however, for tariff purposes, it is only *one* and that *one* classification is the one that determines the *rate of duty* as well as the regulations to which imports and exports are subject.

Importers want the classification that will yield the lowest duty rate. Customs wants the classification that will yield the highest (although, presumably, customs only wants the *correct* classification to be used) amount of money. Thus, commodity classification uncertainty causes problems at the border as well.

Just what is classification and why is it the third bump that is most frequently encountered in the ICC survey I referred to earlier? As mentioned earlier classification is the nomenclature of trade. Classification conveys to border authorities what something is, specifically for tariff, regulatory, and security purposes. An invoice that lists a trade name (e.g., "Brillo") or technical term (e.g., "D(-)-2-Amino-4-phosphonobutyric acid") is meaningless to a customs official trying to determine duty.

To resolve this, an international convention known as the Harmonized System exists that is used by most countries. There will be more on this in the section on Import Process. Failing to use recognized nomenclature is going to cause a problems.

Importers are not typically familiar with the rigorous determination of customs classification. This is done by customs brokers or consultants and recorded on the import (or export) declaration. How these experts determine classification is important to note. The trader (the exporter or the importer) must provide sufficient information to the broker to enable proper classification. This might be in the form of marketing or advertising material, monologues, technical papers, chemical analysis or other documents that describe both the use and makeup of the article. Unless the article is commonplace and is fully recognizable without explanation, it is the trader's responsibility to inform the broker comprehensively and to keep record of the discussion and materials used for reference.

Unnecessary Physical Exams

No one likes to be stopped by a policeman on the road or a customs agent at an airport. Unless you are in the middle of a crime or otherwise wanted by law enforcement, you resolve the issue and move on.

What happens when it is the first order to or from Ho Chi Min City and it is sitting in a Vietnamese customs compound? Whatever the reason for the interdiction—it may be random or targeted because the invoice value is suspect or the nomenclature is Martian or Vietnamese customs have never heard of the company. You may be thousands of miles away and removed from the action and you are not aware that the interdiction has occurred.

When goods are stopped at distant places for whatever reason, all sorts of bad things can happen. The goods can be pilfered or they can be exposed to excessive heat, cold or rain. They can be infiltrated by vermin or nibbled on by rats. They might be stored besides a noxious or even poisonous substance, catch fire or be smashed by some errant forklift. I recall one customs compound where I found my client's medical supplies covered by bird droppings.

It is vital that you know that goods have arrived at the customer or that have not arrived and if not arrived where they are. Every trader should have a system of follow up to make positive determination of the whereabouts of goods.

If goods are interrupted in transit, particularly at a border, it is important but difficult to resolve the issue quickly. The customs broker at destination is probably not too well equipped to accomplish this only because they are not very familiar with the goods or the company. The broker only has the documents to work with. The resolution of delays at foreign customs is going to depend on your customer or affiliate and their relationship with local authorities.

It is difficult to explain to a border officer that stopping the shipment is unnecessary. You are an honest trader and just want to clear up the matter and move on. Not everyone is an honest trader and not everywhere are ethical and moral standards the same. In some places around the world, "tea money" is paid to expedite resolution of delays or inquiries or just to move the papers to the top of the pile. It is not a lot of money; that is why it is called tea money. Another term for tea money is bribe.

Western public companies and their suppliers, increasingly global companies, are forbidden to pay bribes. Private companies may not have the same regulators looking over their shoulder but probably do not want to become part of the border facilitation payroll either. It is hard to stop once you start and paying or even offering a bribe can land you in jail so be very careful with this temptation.

In any case, the object is to avoid interdiction in the first place. While there may be no sure way to do that, one can minimize the likelihood by getting it right in the first place. For example, take steps to assure that the documents covering the transaction are letter perfect—recognized trade terms are used, the parties are all mentioned, the commercial invoice is certified, and other required documents that may be required, such as certificates of origin, travel along with the import country's requirements.

There are many places to get information about what documents are required. Google search "country import requirements" and the results will have a list of the documents. Some of the larger Logistics Service Providers (LSPs) provide this on a commodity-by-commodity basis as well on their websites. UPS, DHL, and FedEx all do as well.

The best source of information is the importer (your customer). It must be presumed that if you are selling a particular good to a company that it knows enough about the good to determine what documents, protocols and possible problems might be encountered. If they do not know – they are unlikely to be a very good partner.

It is helpful to work with shipping agents (foreign freight forwarders), that are familiar with and have a presence on the ground in the importing country and, ideally, have specific expertise in the commodity. This is particularly important if one is trading a highly regulated good, such as an agricultural product or medicine.

In the hypothetical Vietnamese case mentioned above, the best way to resolve interdictions is by working with a customs house broker on the ground that is familiar to local officials. They know who to call for what purpose and they may even be related to the customs officer. I know of many retired customs officials who have subsequently become brokers or consultants themselves.

The border clearance business is like any other human activity. Knowing people helps get things done. When I was in the freight-forwarding industry in Port Elizabeth, our office had a Christmas party every year at a local bar/restaurant in the port area. Law enforcement occupied one side of the room, longshoremen another, customs folks another and we, in the freight business, were on the other side. There was not a lot of kissing and hugging but we knew each other and when we needed help, we had a name to call. That should not be underestimated. As, for example, when the receiving gate for a ship sailing in three hours is closed but my customer must get his container aboard, knowing who to call helps.

In preparation for this topic, I wondered how an SME might avoid the pitfalls of being "unknown." Being "unknown" presents special problems for exporters and importers, including problems related to security. Every reasonable person wants to avoid dealing with a terrorist about to commit a heinous act or a smuggler avoiding authorities or even a human trafficker. Is there a way to avoid the problem of being an "unknown"?

I called a customs friend and asked him that question. From a customs point of view, how would an SME become known, at least "*more known*". His advice was to visit customs at the port of entry and inform them that they will be seeing your company's goods at their port. Unless you are General Motors, that might be difficult, I said.

I recall an IBM executive who did just that. It was his practice to regularly visit countries to which IBM shipped and to meet the local customs man in charge. We are not all IBM and that may not even be economically possible but if it is an important market for your business, it does not hurt to try to visit customs and/or the local chamber of commerce in order to hear directly what can preemptively be done to help the process go smoothly.

You may wish to arrange this through your customer, supplier, or with a local customs agent on the ground. Typically buyers (importers) are responsible for the customs interface. Nevertheless up-front cooperation is better than arguing later about who is at fault for border problems. At the end of the day, it's your business that's at stake.

How Securing the Borders Impacts SMEs

While we are on the subject of the "known" and "unknown shipper," it is relevant to note that security is a special topic, especially since 9-11. There is a special sensitivity with regard to the possibility of chemical, biological, or

10

nuclear weapons (WMD) being transported in commercial trade containers. Not just in America, but worldwide.

Security officials use a variety of tools to detect possible threats, for example, the country of origin of a shipment can raise the threat threshold. However, one that SMEs and infrequent traders face most is the threat that arises from being "unknown." If this is your first shipment coming to Chicago from a trader in Yemen, assume that it is going to get special attention.

Theoretically the first line of defense in interdiction of contraband should be the carrier moving the good as they are presumed to "know" who the shipper and/or the consignee are. In many countries the logistics service provider is required to take proactive steps to assure the identity of the shipper and the cargo itself. Nevertheless, customs officers are incrementally going to pay special attention to consignments from parties they have not seen before. The possibility of this kind of delay should be factored into the planning shipments become more regular and the parties are better "known". Especially in the case of air freight and express shipments, allow an extra three or four days in the planning for transit.

However, do not leave it at that. If the shipment must absolutely arrive at the location by a certain date, take special facilitative steps—especially if it is a one-time or first-time shipment. You might, as an example, call the freight forwarder and tell the person that the shipment needs special tracking. You might mark your documents "urgent," and send your consignee advance emails requesting confirmation of delivery by a certain date. What you do not want to do is to let that special shipment fall into the hopper.

You do not want to be the person who complains to try and get their way. If every third one of your shipments is urgent, to the world, *none of your shipments are urgent*! The company causing trouble, being unreasonable, and raising alarms for everything does not help make for efficient international shipping.

We will return to security in the section on *trusted traders*. Next, we address shipping/transportation because, without it, nothing moves in business.

Part II - Logistics Getting Goods Shipped

The global transportation system gets your company's goods to where they need to go despite enormous complexities. In some ways, global transportation is like traversing an obstacle course. Many thing can go wrong and anything can happen. I recall the chaos that happened a few years ago when a volcano in Iceland brought the European transportation network to a standstill. Who could have anticipated a volcano?

Transportation around the world is not consistent. Even within one country, the availability of predictable shipping is widely varied. Take, for example, in India, the road and rail networks in many rural areas of the country, are undeveloped. Then there is New York City at rush hour. It can take less time to get between La Guardia and Washington than across Broadway at Forty-Fifth Street. Regardless of the state of economic development   transportation problems exist everywhere because of the enormous number of packages being shipped in every direction, in every mode, every day and everywhere.

Typically, the "final kilometer," which is the delivery phase from or to a factory or port, is both the costliest and the most challenging. It is usually the responsibility of the buyer (on imports) to get from the port to the warehouse and the seller's responsibility (on exporters) to get from the warehouse to the port.

Who has what role is specified in the agreed-upon terms. For example, the term "Ex Works" means that the goods are sold at the factory or warehouse door and the buyer is responsible for the costs and risks beyond. (see *Incoterms* below). In the USA the term more commonly used is f.o.b. (free on board). The f.o.b. point determines transfer of title and responsibility for making transport arrangements.

Getting to or from the foreign port (port to port) is typically that portion of logistics cost and service that will affect the viability of the business most. An understanding of the transportation industry is key to SME competitiveness or failure.

In the simplest sense, transportation is about getting a widget from point A to point B. In the real world, nothing is that simple. Widgets are picked up somewhere, moved somewhere else by another carrier, transferred again to yet another carrier, and possibly, to a fourth or fifth carrier. The inter-line between those links can be smooth and efficient or not. Much will depend on five essential factors in addition to a basic understanding of how things work:

- Rate elasticity

- Volume

- Direction of travel

- Density

- Nature of the product

- Mode of shipping

Sensitivity to Shipping Costs

Rate elasticity is the cargo's sensitivity to rates. Folks in the business say this is "what the traffic will bear." When something is sold, the "landed cost" is the sum of both the goods and the expenses related to the logistics. Incrementally, this number starts with the value of the goods (known as "Ex-works"—EXW) plus the freight and forwarding ("cost and freight"—C&F), cargo insurance (Cost, Insurance & Freight—CIP), and delivery costs to the customer's warehouse, including customs, duty, and formalities (Delivered Duty Paid— DDP, also known as "free domicile").

Total cost is a very fundamental concept. The price of the good itself is irrelevant if the cost of shipping is higher than the market is willing to pay and the seller is unwilling to absorb. That is what is meant by *what the traffic will bear.* Clearly, expensive wrist watches can withstand a higher logistics cost than a box of cereal. Even wrist watches will not "move" at a certain total cost. When negotiating for freight services, it is important to understand that "how much the traffic will bear" is a fundamental factor in the negotiation of rates, fees, and service expectations with service providers.

In the case of goods sold for export, the final cost to the consumer includes distribution costs in-country and perhaps VAT (Value Added Tax). Starting with market price, a person may work backward to determine whether the business is viable while recognizing that the major costs of logistics are not fixed.

How sensitive the business model is to shipping and related costs is as fundamental a question going forward as determining manufacturing cost of goods or, if you are sourcing from foreign countries, transportation is as important to determine the feasibility of the source as the vendor's ex-works price. Many a procurement manager has been unhappily surprised to discover that landed cost is significantly higher than planned. This is because the manager's narrow focus on the ex-works (or f.o.b. factory) price loses sight of the fact that the goods need to be delivered.

One of the reasons transportation is often difficult to estimate more accurately, especially during the startup of operations, is that those costs are a function of many factors. At the top of the list of those is *volume*.

1. How much will be shipped (weight and cube) at a time?

2. Over what period of time?

3. Between the same places (ports)?

4. In a particular mode (e.g., air cargo)?

Those factors, together with rate sensitivity, make the business attractive or not to the service provider. If it is many large shipments of high value (rate insensitive) cargoes, then it will be more attractive than making a few shipments of low-value goods.

Knowing where business fits in that spectrum will enable you to understand how the business is perceived by potential providers of service and that is the first step in negotiating shipping rates.

There was a time when all similarly situated shippers had to be treated the same, without discrimination regarding rates and service. Today, in most of the world, that is no longer the case. The business exists in an essentially deregulated shipping market where the revenue potential you represent becomes a very compelling factor in your ability to successfully survive from a logistical point of view. That is such an important concept that it is necessary to define in logistical terms exactly what an SME is.

What Is an SME for Logistical Purposes?

I said in the previous section that "volume" is a compelling factor. The term volume has two aspects: 1) frequency; and 2) amount measured in freight terms. If you make one shipment a year, that is infrequent unless the shipment is a planeload of electronic equipment that is going to generate a lot of revenue to the chosen service provider.

By the same reasoning, if you ship one small, low-valued parcel to the same place every week, that might be considered high frequency but low volume and not very attractive, depending on the mode. If that one parcel happens to pay a lot of freight (for example art work), that becomes very attractive.

That concept (frequency x amount x rate) is useful in considering "who" you are best positioned to negotiate logistics services. That is because just as there are SME traders, there are SME service providers.

One small weekly shipment might be a big customer to a small freight forwarder even though it will not appear significant to a giant ocean carrier moving thousands of 20-foot containers on every ship. You want to estimate what your spend is going to be over a period (see above) so that you can intelligently scout out service providers to whom you will be as attractive a customer as possible. Picking up the phone and calling the first freight company that shows up in a Google search is probably not going to yield the best relationship.

As a buyer of services, you want to be attractive as a potential customer. Having a realistic estimate of the potential annual spend will enable you to position the business attractively to *someone*. A national account executive with a book of customers in the millions might not find an SME very interesting. An ambitious young salesman might. A major steamship company may not have a lot of interest in your quarterly 20-foot container but a consolidator of containers might!

Given your estimated spend, to whom is the company a big customer? That is the objective. An extension of that is *who is able to provide the service needed.*

It is fundamental to understand that cost is not the compelling factor in growing a business if the logistics of customer service is inadequate. What can be worse than a low airfare on an airline that cancels and delays flights?

The single most important factor in supply chain management is reliability. Low cost is only useful if it can maintain an adequate level of service to the customers. That means that goods have to arrive on time and in good condition and people need to be available to answer questions when needed. *If you fail to measure and monitor this, you will most certainly fail!*

I have known and worked for many companies that think the function of measuring service is over when the truck is loaded or the plane takes off. It is not, no matter what the terms of the sale.

Finding the right size provider is enabled by networking at export- and import-oriented trade groups. Such groups exist in many cities and attending periodically is important for the topical content and to network with similar traders. Invariably, you will find more service providers selling than shippers buying. Consider this a learning opportunity. In my own career, as both a buyer and seller of transportation services, I made my best connections at trade association meetings.

Next, let us look more closely at the underlying providers of transportation.

Freight Rates

Regular route common carriers (truckers, airlines, vessel operators) have large capital investments in plant and equipment, ergo high fixed costs. Covering those costs is a very big deal. The larger the investment, the more important regular traffic becomes. As expected, those companies rely on large commitments of regular traffic to cover fixed costs.

The typical SME does not represent a "base" cargo opportunity. Base cargo is the steady traffic that pays the high fixed cost. Asset-based carriers need to pay the fixed cost even if the rate charged is low for the market. Base cargo comes from the largest regular shippers. If the business can be a consistent shipper you

16

should look for long-term contractual relationships that will promise the carrier the traffic and enable an optimized freight cost.

At the same time consider the marginal cost to an ocean carrier of carrying *one more container* aboard an 8,000-container vessel. Not much. It is basically the handling costs on the shore. The consequence is the carrier may view the shipment opportunistically and agree to a bargain price. The SME with even a small volume of regular traffic can exploit marginal pricing opportunities, especially where competition exists in lanes of traffic characterized by huge shipping company competitors.

What about the *really* small trader? If there is no significant spend, the small company may not have any significant negotiating leverage. The remaining options all entail paying the highest price for transportation. The first question becomes "can the traffic bear the cost of transportation?" If yes, then the express carriers, such as DHL, UPS, and FedEx provide strong services, even for the SME.

It is service capability that the product requires and those providers become essential to success with services such as track-and-trace capability needed for customer service, clearance, security, and other strengths maintained for all customers, including the small ones. The small shipment moves along with all of the other freight and thus, benefits.

What is important for the very small shipper to realize is that <u>until sufficient volume is generated to enable price and service customization, the business must support high transportation and logistics costs.</u>

The question to get answered is "will the business model support shipping costs over the long term?"

Direction

Before I left the freight forwarding business, I was able to move freight in twenty-foot containers from the East Coast of the United States to California for an aggressively priced $50 per container. Yet, I could not take a cab ride from the west to the east side of New York City for $50. How was this possible? It was possible because of the direction of traffic.

Freight, then and today, moves in great volume from Asia to North America and Europe. Carriers (both surface and marine) need to get their equipment back to Asia for more freight. They are sometimes willing to accept almost anything to underwrite at least some part the "backhaul." That is why the cost of shipping correlates to the direction of the traffic.

Transportation is essentially a supply-and-demand business. Where demand is high and supply is scarce, rates shoot up. Where demand is weak and supply is plentiful, rates drop lower the cost. If the business is shipping-cost sensitive, locating sources of supply in the opposite direction from the major flow of traffic can make a big economic difference. Depending on what percentage of total cost goes to shipping, logistics costs can be more important than production costs (EXW). In addition to which, competition for regular traffic in backhaul networks will help to assure the highest level of customer service.

Not surprisingly, the opposite of all of this is also true. During peak seasons, such as summers before the Christmas shopping season in the West and immediately before or after threatened work stoppages, the demand for space on ships and airplanes soars. Large shippers with firm contracted space get on those conveyances first, along with lucrative, high-paying cargoes. Everyone else follows, or is just left behind until "the large companies" are accommodated.

The SMEs have few options. If the company is an infrequent shipper of low-paying freight, then it is not going to get service. There are strategies that can be employed that seek to make the business appear as a larger shipper. For example, using a piggyback tactic.

Let us say you are an exporter and your customer is a large company (for example, Walmart or Marks & Spencer). It might work for both parties to sell goods without the freight. An example of this would be an Argentine manufacturer selling to a Walmart f.a.s. ("free alongside"). In this case, Walmart's greater purchasing leverage can minimize freight costs and assure service.

The same logic applies to the SME importer. If the manufacturer or supplier is a large company, it will be able to secure lower costs and better service and the business will become a "dual" customer of the service provider along with the exporter.

If the company is considering overseas expansion, such as a new service or distribution center location, it may want to ask whether it can locate the center in a favorable backhaul location.

Density

All transportation conveyances are constrained by physical limitations. Doors are of a limited size, cranes capable of much weight, boxes only big enough for many cubic centimeters. Every unit of freight-carrying capacity has to <u>at least</u> contribute to the absorption of cost (fixed and variable).

A common term for units of freight is "freight ton." A freight ton has two dimensions, cubic displacement ("cube") and weight. Thus, even the largest vessel has both a limited cubic capacity and a weight capacity, whichever comes first. If the weight exceeds weight capacity, the ship sinks. The airplane falls. Excessive cube cannot fit at all, no matter how light in weight.

Cargo that is bulkier per cubic meter than it is heavy is rated per measurement ton in sea transportation and by weight ton if it is heavier than bulky per cubic meter. A metric ton in sea transportation is 1,000 kilos or cubic meters. A short ton in the United States is 2,000 pounds. A freight ton will be Imperial 2,000 pounds or 40 cubic feet, whichever yields the greater revenue.

There is a similar system for airfreight. "Chargeable" weight (also known as volume-metric) is calculated as 6,000 cubic meters per kilo, (166 cubic inches to the pound).

Transportation rates are always per chargeable weight (weight or measure). Sometimes the rate for a specific commodity or class of commodities is only quoted by the carrier in weight terms. However In determining the rate that will apply to the specific commodity or category of commodities, the transportation company has taken the density of the commodity into account.

Packaging

Given that freight cost is directly related to density (weight per cubic displacement), packaging takes on a lot of importance. Every "freight ton" (weight or measured ton) contributes to freight cost. Thus, the more dense the package, the less the cost per unit of product contained.

Consider bubble packaging. Sometimes, a small widget is shipped in a big box. To limit movement damage, the box is filled with bubble wrap. That makes the package bigger and the cost to ship the contained widget increases! A total waste of money.

Similarly, pallets are a good labor-saving device that adds a level of protection. But sometimes, cartons or cargo on pallets sit in the middle of the pallet with a lot of wasted space around. The measure of the shipment on a pallet is not just the cube of the cartons but the pallet squared off. The more dense the pallet, the less the cost of shipping each unit on the pallet.

The same applies to freight containers. They are a great way to ship cargo. They reduce theft and reduce contact with other obnoxious freight and movement damage. Just like a ship, a truck, or an airplane, a freight container has a cubic capacity and a weight capacity. Often containers are not fully utilized and sometimes, only 50% or 60%% is utilized. There may be a good reason to do this but the cost per unit of freight is twice as high as it would be if the container is fully utilized. That is especially the case when the transportation is quoted per container, per trip, and per unit load device (ULD).

The message is that the SME will optimize the transportation cost by making the packaging as dense as possible, consistent with the safety of the commodity. Is the product packaged to minimize transportation costs?

Nature of the Product

The nature of the commodity being shipped is a fundamental issue in international shipping. Fragile; temperature-sensitive; time-sensitive; dangerous; obnoxious; extra length, height, or wide cargoes all require special handling and may require special permits to be exported, imported, or to travel on public roads or conveyances such as commercial airplanes. They directly affect the mode of transportation that is used.

Hazardous Material

The cheapest mode of transportation may simply not be available to the company! For example, highly flammable goods may be prohibited from air transport except in very small quantities ("limited quantities"). This even applies to consumer goods such as fragrances. If importing or exporting flammable consumer products such as perfumes, and the quantities are too small for sea freight, then the exporter must assure that that packaging meets the quantity limitation per package and other rules that apply to shipping flammable commodities by air cargo. The International Air Transport Association (IATA) promulgates rules regarding dangerous cargoes by air freight. If shipping those, then see the link below.

http://www.iata.org/whatwedo/cargo/dgr/Pages/index.aspx

Please note: one cannot ship dangerous goods by any mode, especially air freight, without assuring compliance with the applicable rules. It will cost more for freight. That is the business the company is in and thus cannot be avoided.

I recall a freight consolidator who had a great business. He specialized in the movement of dangerous goods. Since he was a specialist, his customers understood how he could charge less than anyone else! He was an expert! What he actually did was stuff hazmats in the nose of sea freight containers and then fill the tail with ordinary, non-hazardous cargo. He paid the shipping lines a lump sum FAK ("freight all kinds") non-hazardous cargo rate for his boxes. He retailed the transportation to less than full-load shippers at lower LCL ("less than container load") rates than others charged and made a nice profit. His rates were lower, his costs were based on non-hazardous transportation and his sales rates were based on dangerous goods. He spent time in **jail** and the sale of his house just about covered the fine.

What Happens at Borders Physically?

International transportation is about getting goods from one country to another by air, sea, truck, or rail. Often, multiple modes are employed to accomplish the transit. For example, the truck from the supplier to the airport, the aircraft from airport to airport, and the truck from the airport to the customer.

Usually, the shipper is not aware of the interactions between transport companies. The end-to-end transportation seems seamless. In fact, it is not seamless and it is not without risk. For example, the truck that picks up will deliver the goods to a terminal or "cross docking" facility, where the cargo is moved into queue according to destination, where it can become misplaced. As with luggage, a parcel can get into the wrong queue and on the wrong airplane or simply fail to make a connection. Even railroad cars can be "way laid" and find themselves in the wrong city.

Modern transport companies use Bar Code readers and Radio Frequency Identification (RFID) tags affixed to parcels to keep track of goods while they move from conveyance to conveyance. A layering of data enables the tracking of hundreds of packages. For example, a box is on a pallet, a pallet is in a freight container, a freight container is on a flat car, and a flat car is on a train. By reading the bar code or RFID affixed to the lead car, we can determine where any particular parcel is. Often, this remote communications is accomplished by satellite tracking systems.

Even with sophisticated technologies, items are lost. The ability of the service providers to provide "track and trace" capability, either on its own or through the carriers it engages on your behalf, is an important consideration.

The process has two aspects that must be synchronized- the movement of the goods and the movement of the documentation about the goods. This can be described, (in simplified terms) as follow: Goods are picked up at the shipping point and delivered to a vessel. At about the same time documents are generated by the exporter (e.g. invoices, packing lists, instructions) and sent (by email or other means) to a freight forwarder that prepares bills of lading and export declarations and delivers them to the ocean carrier. When the goods are "received" at the ocean terminal the carrier releases a (rated) waybill that goes back to the forwarder.

(The carrier has its own internal processes based on the cargo booking and bills of lading. For example, the carrier prepares a load plan detailing where cargo is to be stowed and cargo manifests for customs and other purposes).

The shipment is now on its way to the destination. "Overhead" the forwarder sends completed documents (e.g. freight is added to the commercial invoice) to the customer's custom broker at the destination. The broker receives the documents and completes an import declaration delivered to local customs (typically this is done electronically).

Customs processes the declaration and (if there are no issues) sends the ocean carrier a "release" so that when the vessel arrives the broker can arrange for the cargo to be picked up from the piers and delivered to the consignee.

Customs processing includes scanning the declaration (and manifest) for potential security threats. If other participating agencies have jurisdiction (such as agriculture authorities) they are notified as well.

When cargo arrives customs and "other participating agencies" may or may not decide to detain the shipment for inspection. This might be a comparison of the import declaration to the physical cargo to assure the declaration is truthful and accurate. Agriculture authorities may inspect for insects or evidence of fumigation if that is required. Health may inspect to assure medicaments are admissible.

If a routine inspection is successful the cargo is released to the trucker picking up the consignment for delivery to the consignee. If problems are detected by border authorities the process can take an indefinite an unpredictable length of time to resolve. Part VI describes numbers examples of these kinds of frustrating delays.

The "takeaway" is that internationally, freight moves on two parallel planes. The cargo itself moves physically from the origin warehouse to a port and then onto the destination port, where it is picked up and delivered onward. At the same time, there is a paper/data flow. At every step there is the possibility of a problem.

Importers and exporters may be unable, even unaware, of problems that may occur in the logistical process. What you can do is not contribute to causing them.

Typically the exporter prepares commercial documents and sends them to a freight forwarder before the forwarder books cargo or arranges transport to the vessel. Sometimes, shippers fail to do this and goods arrive at terminals or truck terminals in port areas and cannot be identified. This is a particularly difficult problem in "nearby foreign" shipments where cargo arrives at destination in a few days. If the shipper is tardy getting commercial documents to the forwarder, the forwarder cannot get the documents to the consignee with the result that shipments cannot be cleared and become subject to demurrage (storage) charges.

As indicated the broker prepares import declarations for customs and, if needed, other regulators, and obtains clearance to proceed with the delivery. This may necessitate the payment of duty or the guarantee (a bond) to pay the duty and VAT. Inaccurate information, such as a discrepancy in piece count (the number of boxes in the consignment) can cause delay. Insufficient information to make a definite customs classification can cause delay. Failing to provide registration information for medicines will cause delay.

The lesson is any variation from what is expected or between what is declared and what actually is observable can cause difficult to resolve issues.

If no issues arise at customs the broker typically follows the buyer's instructions regarding final delivery. The broker prepares another document that is sent to a trucker who then goes to the pier or airport, picks up the cargo, and delivers it to the buyer.

This process occurs on both sea and air shipments. The difference in mode is that documents generally travel with the cargo in air freight and contiguous surface shipments.

Given the clearance process cannot proceed without the exporter's documents (data), these should arrive at destination before the freight (or simultaneously in air cargo). Often, documents do not arrive before or simultaneous with the cargo. "Freight no papers" and "papers no freight" are not uncommon with consequent delays.

Until the two flows (data and freight) synchronize, the consignment cannot be delivered.

What Mode?

By mode, I refer to the means of transportation—air cargo, sea freight, express, motor, rail. (Pipe transportation is another modality but I suspect not one for the SME).

It is a general rule that the cheapest mode is by water (including barge) and the most expensive is air cargo. The selection depends on service commitment to the customer for exports and imports. If the promise is fresh Colombian produce or flowers delivered every morning in Tokyo or Rome, sea freight is not an option.

Similarly, if the service requirement is to deliver a replacement part within 24 hours to a customer in Seattle from a service center in Dublin, even standard air freight is not going to work. If the commitment is to deliver tee shirts from Haiti to Liverpool 60 days from receipt of the order, air freight will be too costly and there is plenty of time for sea transport.

The selection of mode begins with an understanding of service commitment to the market. Amazon and Alibaba have made deliveries in a very short time from ordering a cornerstone of their business. Companies are considering the use of drones for faster delivery to the door of the customer. Germany is testing strategically placed kiosks to hold those products most sensitive to consumer immediate gratification.

Both Amazon and Alibaba understand that logistics cost must necessarily be factored in to pricing. Huge companies such as Amazon and retailers depend on their tremendous volume to negotiate preferential transportation rates, which they are able to retail as part of a membership or in the shipping cost add-on. Whether shipping is part of the price in membership arrangements or added on to the cost of the item, freight has been carefully considered. The consumer benefits from the enormous purchasing leverage of these huge buyers of logistics services.

The important point is that the cost of service commitment is factored into the business model. Service and cost are intertwined.

The first step in developing a strategic plan is deciding what the service commitment must be to sustain the business plan. *For example, I will* <u>*deliver*</u> *to my customer within 24 hours of receipt of order no matter where he is located.* It all starts there. Knowing the service commitment enables a reasoned analysis of transportation options.

<u>It is possible that no option exists to support the business model.</u> One cannot ship goods for free. It may be that only a local business or exports or imports from an adjacent market are sustainable. It is best to make an objective determination before jumping into distant markets.

For most SMEs, the two most important types of service provider are foreign freight forwarders and custom house brokers. Freight forwarders are travel agents for freight. Custom house brokers are analogous to tax form preparers.

Foreign Freight Forwarders

Freight forwarders make arrangements for exportations, including transportation. In some countries, they are licensed; in other countries, the forwarding fee is determined by the government. Freight forwarders are experts in international shipping and documentation, having learned the trade either on the job or formally.

German and Dutch forwarders are considered professionals, similar to a CPA or a chartered accountant. In the USA individuals are licensed as brokers and must pass a very difficult written test. Freight forwarders as companies are licensed but as individuals learn their trade "on the job".

Forwarders attend to many border formalities, such as filing export declarations with authorities and submitting collection documents to banks. They book cargo with transport providers (carriers) and arrange for cargo insurance. Freight forwarders are selected by the exporter who uses the same service provider for all of his business. The importer may nominate the forwarder for the same reason. Both the seller and the buyer want freight forwarders who are familiar with their business needs.

There are advantages and disadvantages to both. Increasingly, governments are requiring advance information to be electronically submitted and penalties may be imposed if the data are inaccurate or late. If the freight forwarder is the seller's agent, it may not be familiar with the importer's regulatory requirements or be as responsive. This can negatively impact the importer. The importer may be using the freight forwarder (overseas) to consolidate shipments into larger consignments in order to save money on freight or to expedite shipments when working with vendors. When an importer (buyer) selects the forwarder from the origin country, it is doing so to increase control over its logistics.

However there is a potential disadvantage for the seller in allowing the buyer selecting the forwarder. The primary disadvantage is loss of control and possibility of diversion, especially in the case of branded goods or where market agreements restrict the buyer to a limited geographic market. When control of the transport is ceded to the buyer's forwarder, the result may be that goods are sold back into the seller's own market or another distributor's territory. That is referred to as "gray market." The other risk is that the goods may wind up being diverted to a denied party or a sanctioned country, which could expose the seller to significant perils.

The extent to which criminals will go to profit on lack exporter controls cannot be underestimated. I recall the case of a large consumer products company whose expired beauty product was tendered to a disposal company for burial. The goods were later dug up and sold through discount stores.

Even when the seller retains control by selecting its own forwarder, there is still risk of *diversion*. There are countless cases of goods being shipped to a foreign port and then being reloaded and returned to the seller's domestic market. I worked with another consumer products company who delivered a particularly saleable beauty aid to Italy. The Italian buyer never cleared customs. The goods were shipped back to New York in the very same freight containers, without ever unloading.

Diversion is a important additional reason to "know your customer", especially if your goods have a significant potential for diversion. Some companies believe that dual language or special markings on consumer packages will block diversion. Not necessarily. There are numerous cases of specially marked, even dual language, products being marketed back in the exporter's country through discounters and other means.

From a strategic point of view, the decision as to who should engage the logistics service provider/forwarder should encompass consideration of the risks and the benefits involved. If you are selling directly to a consumer, there is no reason why the buyer should want to select the forwarder. If you are the buyer, you may want the additional control yourself so this is a point of negotiation.

As an SME, you may want to leverage your volume as much as possible or you may want to cede control to the exporter (seller) because it is the larger company and is capable of procuring better service at a lower cost. Although this may be a decision made on a customer-by-customer basis, a strategic philosophy that will drive individual decisions is a good practice.

The main goal is minimizing cost in order to lower price or stretch profit. It pays to determine, objectively, who benefits from forwarder selection, your company or your customer?

Air Freight

Air freight is controlled by air freight forwarders located at airports. They receive cargo, schedule the cargo aboard airlines, mark, label and unitize the cargo (put it on pallets or air freight containers called ULDs), complete the export documents, cut and air the waybill, and deliver the freight to the airline, all ready to go.

In the United States, some of these companies are designated as certified cargo security screening facilities. They check to ensure that the cargo is not being used for terrorism purposes.

Air freight forwarders either own the airplanes (such as UPS and DHL) or they contract airline space. The difference between the rate at which they buy space and the rate at which they sell to you is the gross profit. There are certain commission arrangements that are based on hitting certain volume targets.

There may be additional handling charges, such as pick up from your warehouse and a fee for preparing bank documents or consular legalization of your papers.

There are very large global forwarders with offices and terminals in various countries. There are also many small companies that specialize in one market, such as Italy or Greece. Since the profitability of a forwarder depends on its "buy" rate with the airline, it must generate consistent volume.

The large forwarders (also known as logistics service providers) generally do this by contracting with the large international shippers. The smaller forwarders generate volume by specializing in specific markets where they have particularly reliable contacts. One forwarder I worked with had very knowledgeable agents in Africa so our company was the most competitive, even against the largest forwarders.

The selection of air freight forwarders for specific trade lanes can afford more aggressive rate negotiations. For example, if you ship regularly from Milan to New York, you will be a large shipper to a regional forwarder than to a global forwarder for whom your volume may be insignificant.

Regarding ULDs, just as in sea freight, these types of containers afford cargo greater protection than shipping goods loose, or even on pallets. They can be configured to maintain temperatures for 48-72 hours and some even longer. Generally, they are not loaded at the shipper's premises, although that is possible. Cargo is generally delivered to the forwarder at the airport and it does the unitizing, either into "cans" or on to pallets that are configured to the shape of the aircraft to be used. As with sea freight ("nvos"), freight forwarders consolidate the freight of many shippers into those to achieve lower buy rates.

Integrators

The other fast transit option (across oceans), especially for the shipment of parcels, is the integrator. Those firms can provide "door-to-door" transport and, in some cases, even arrange for border clearance for consignments of limited invoice value.

"Express" companies, such as DHL, UPS, and FedEx, specialize in this type of service and may represent excellent logistical options, especially where shipments go to many different customers in one or multiple countries. An integrator can come into your facility once a day or once a month and pick up all available shipments. Those can be traced by you or by your customer electronically.

The cost of express services is high on a per-kilo basis but low compared with making multiple transport arrangements. For example, to ship a 2-kilo box in the conventional way would incur a minimum charge to pick up the parcel, a minimum air freight charge, a minimum "final mile" charge, and fixed fees for freight forwarding and custom house brokerage.

Custom House Brokers

Brokers are domiciled in the importing country and are appointed by the buyer. Brokers file official declarations in the name of the importer and are "attorney in fact." Brokers receive documents from the exporter or his or her forwarder and use them, along with instructions from the importer, to complete and file import declarations.

Import declarations are the basis for admission (admissibility) and for the appraisal of goods for the purpose of collecting duties and taxes. Special documents may be needed to satisfy "other government agency" requirements. For example, agricultural goods may require special certificates. Medicines may require separate declarations.

More than the work performed by freight forwarders, custom house brokerage is highly sensitive to regulatory compliance issues. The commodities must be according to the national tariff (see "harmonized system" above).

The value must be the true value, which broadly means that the prices declared are arm's length pricing, between unrelated buyers and without other payments of any sort before or after filing the declaration. As indicated earlier, royalties and equipment supplied to the seller to manufacture the article are examples of payments that do not usually appear on the seller's invoices. It is your responsibility to assure your broker is aware of all of the payments made or to be made that do not appear on the commercial invoice.

The origin country of the goods must be declared even if that is not the same country as the country from which the goods are shipped. For example, goods may have been manufactured in Korea and then shipped to Mexico for packaging although the preponderance of value was made in Korea. In this example, special trade agreements may exist between Mexico and the buyer's country, which might provide for duty elimination. Declaring that the goods are Mexican when they are actually the produce of Korea would be wrong and might possibly result in fines, penalties, and worse.

It is noteworthy that even origin is not necessarily interpreted by all government agencies in the same way. For example, one agency may consider the country in which a product is finished (e.g. packaged for retail sale) completed as the origin while another agency may consider the country of origin the place where the good took on its essential characteristics. Yet another may consider the origin the country where an agricultural good is grown (product of) versus where it is packaged.

Whether you are buying or selling goods internationally you need to know the origin of your goods for customs and other agency purposes in order to assure declarations are properly made. I have known of cases where customs have picked up boxes marked with a country of origin where the import declaration says another, this is common. It demonstrates a failure of internal communication.

Declaring the correct commodity, value, and origin are three key elements of a transaction that must be truthful and correct. There are others. In order for a broker to correctly file declarations, it must be completely familiar with the importer's commodities and business model. It is inadequate to send a broker shipping documents and expect that the broker will know how to fill out documents. Since the broker is the attorney in fact, errors and omissions are the importer's errors and omissions.

Clearly, both foreign freight forwarders and custom brokers need to be provided with information and specific instructions. By specific instructions, I mean a written standard operating procedure (SOP)"). In order to ensure compliance with the laws, the SOP should state clearly that the agent is not authorized to make illegal payments in connection with your business (for

31

example, pay bribes to officials). The agent should sign a copy of the SOP and you should retain a copy for in the company files.

Service providers, not the SME, are the experts. You can and should expect expert advice from the service provider. Those two categories of providers should have expertise in your line of products, especially if they are subject to multiple-agency jurisdiction. You would not go to a gastroenterologist for a heart problem. They may both be medical doctors but if the problem is your heart, you want a heart expert. Similarly, your service providers should have specific expertise and other clients in the same or similar business.

There is the fear that your information will be provided to a competitor if the agent handles both accounts. While it may be possible to file a criminal or civil action in court if this happens, the best advice is to know and trust your provider. They are a part of your business. It is very important to clearly spell out expectations.

To summarize, transportation service and related costs can make or break an international business. The key to succeeding is a realistic self-assessment of what your business requires to be competitive in both service and landed cost terms. Thereafter researching and identifying those logistics providers that can accommodate your logistical needs and continuously monitoring that performance is essential.

Part III - Regulatory Hurdles

Synchronizing transportation with paperwork flow is essential but does not assure the avoidance of border delays. On both the export and import side of an international shipment, complex regulatory hurdles must be attended to or the shipment goes nowhere, often without either the exporter or the importer being aware of the delay or even confiscation.

A detailed explanation of the issues and processes involved in crossing jurisdictional borders is beyond the scope of this book. The process of importing medicaments into the United States is a book all by itself. If you are trading highly regulated commodities, you are going to need expert advice and logistics service from providers that have specific expertise.

At a high level, there are those routine processes common to every shipment for export and import.

Export Controls

Routine processes are those that are not specific to either the export country or the final destination or to the commodity being shipped. For example, shipments from the United States to North Korea are banned. At this printing, the EU maintains an embargo on certain goods to Russia. With rare exception, if you have a customer from North Korea and you are subject to American law, or a customer in Russia and you are a European company, you have an issue. If your product has a military or terrorist capability, you have an issue regardless of the ultimate destination.

Martial capabilities include "dual use" possibilities. For example, a drone may be marketed and its intention may be to search for sharks at beaches but can be used to spot soldiers in a combat zone. If you have such an article, you have an issue regardless of the destination. The issue is not what you are selling the item as, the issue is what the article can be used for if it has the <u>potential</u> for martial or suppressive capability.

If you are engaged in international business, it is essential that you are aware of political developments that may impact your business. An example is the joint United States and EU sanction on Russia as a country and on specific individuals within Russia, which resulted from Russia's adventures in the Ukraine. Notice that I said Russia and specific Russian nationals. If your commodity is forbidden, you are subject to criminal prosecution if you sell to either of those "denied" categories.

The phrase commonly used to capture basic diligence regarding export control compliance is "know your customer!" I add to that "know your product!" Does the product have the remotest strategic significance and does it make sense that your prospective customer is ordering it? For example, do you sell high tech tools to measure radioactivity? Can they be used to see in the dark? Or tiny cameras with no consumer application? Is your Bahamas-based customer ordering winter hunting gear? Or is your Swedish prospect interested in desert desert-enabled generators? Those are examples of a mismatch between customers and products.

Does the French customer only have a New York phone number? It is elusive about providing a French address? Does it insist on paying cash? Twenty-five thousand dollars in cash? Those are mismatches between common business practices and the prospect.

Does it insist on making its own shipping arrangements and only provide a warehouse address in Brooklyn as the delivery address? Or offer to pick up goods at your warehouse?

Those and other oddities are "red flags" that something is amiss and you should be on the lookout for them. The link below to ITAR (International Traffic In Arms Regulations) is a handy guide, whether your product is a munition or baby food and whether you are domiciled in Kansas or Katmandu.

http://www.exportrules.com/itar/13-red-flag-indicators-for-export-transactions.html

Third Country Boycotts

It is more than just a good idea to ensure that your field offices and agents are educated in compliance issues and that includes communicating the policies and procedures that you expect them to follow as a condition of doing business.

Red flags is a tool than can be interpreted in the form of a customer service checklist, which you can require your agents and affiliates to follow in soliciting and accepting new business.

It is important to recognize that complying with the laws of your country may not be enough. You may well be responsible for compliance with the regulations your affiliate is subject to in its country as well as yours.

For example, there may be conflicts between local laws and the laws pertaining to third-country sales, which the business is subject to in its country. The affiliate's host country may participate in a third-country embargo but your country may forbid your compliance with that embargo. Such cases compel you to seek legal advice before proceeding and that you communicate your policy to your affiliate or agent.

There is nothing like the appeal of a large sale to tempt sales folks, at home and abroad, from looking the other way, even when something is not right. I have experienced many instances where a great sales opportunity has put temporary blinders on general managers who should have known better. Sometimes these may be a violation of law or corporate policies, but not always. As alluded to earlier I have seen cases of expired product being sold at discounted prices and another of a general manager selling against the company itself.

Whether the company compliance program is about adherence to applicable laws or corporate polices, they are not effective without enforcement, have written policies and a process to check for compliance that is documented and can be independently audited.

Import Process

From the foregoing discussion, one can see the need to question whether there may be a restriction on exporting a commodity. Even if there is no such restriction, there may be a control on the import of a product on the other end.

One example of this is pharmaceutical and medical devices. In most countries, these products require approval and registration with the domestic health agency. In the United States, that is the US Food and Drug Administration

(FDA) and depending on the substance, other agencies such as the Centers for Disease Control and Prevention (CDC), if one is importing an active biological substance, even if it is a small amount for research. If one is exporting a biological from Ireland to Cleveland, they and the importer are going to have to manage issues arising from the FDA and the CDC.

When I was a freight forwarder, it was common to hear exporters take the position that issues related to importation on the other side (import) are the buyer's problem. Not so. The exporter may not be responsible for compliance with the buyer's import laws but if the goods are confiscated or destroyed, the financial implication may make the legal implication moot. Knowing the customer and the product will prevent negative results.

A common pitfall that arises, especially dealing with smaller entities—*a buyer's request that the invoice declares the goods as something other than what they are*. If this happens, you have an issue. It is possible that there is a legitimate need to declare goods a certain way in order to obtain the most favorable customs treatment. For example, the importer may have obtained a customs ruling on the commodity. Or it may be an attempt at fraud.

A customer might ask the seller to falsely declare an item on an invoice in order to circumvent import controls or avoid the payment of customs duty. In this case you are being asked to be complicit in a crime. Moreover, you may have created an export compliance issue if you or your forwarding agent uses the false declaration in the preparation of the required export declaration. This is because the export declaration is subject to the law governing your company, not the overseas customer. What is the appropriate verbiage to use on invoices and other documents in order to avoid border issues?

As indicated, commodity descriptions are fundamental to both the export and import process. We alluded to this earlier in the section on import bumps as classification uncertainty.

On import filings, commodity classifications are used by specialists to make import declarations that determine the applicable rate of duty and for other purposes (such as food and drug compliance). This is done with reference to the international "harmonized system," which most countries have adopted.

If your company is an importer, the brand or trade name of the article must be translated into the corresponding tariff classification as found in the national tariff schedule, which is based on the harmonized system of commodity descriptions.

It is worth taking a little closer look at commodity descriptions because much is determined by which classifications are used in declaration. Classification of goods for customs purposes are found at the global level in a publication of the World Customs Organization called the Harmonized System "HS". HS lists over 5,000 commodities and assigns each one a six-digit HS code.

Trading countries in the world have adopted the HS system at least to the six-digit level. Countries, including the United States, can be more specific in the national tariffs but must be harmonized at the six-digit level. The United States goes to 10 digits. Nevertheless, classifying the widget, even at the six-digit level, makes it possible to achieve some consistency on both the export and the import side and across markets.

HS is arranged meticulously according to groups of commodities into ninety-seven nine-seven chapters ranging from live animals (Chapter 1) to antiques (Chapter 97) with two additional chapters for special national information that does not fit anywhere else neatly. I will use the US version for illustrative purposes, see "Harmonized Tariff Schedule of the United States (2016) Chapter 8, EDIBLE FRUIT AND NUTS; PEEL OF CITRUS FRUIT OR MELONS"

Chapter 8, which covers nuts. the first item, 0801, covers coconuts and 0801.11.00.00 specifies that the item pertains to desiccated nuts, 0801.12 to desiccated nuts in the inner shell. That seems pretty simple. Find the family of things the good falls into then find the specific product. If there is no specific mention, one can fall back on the "not otherwise" specified item closest to under the head note. Does this cover edible nuts? Maybe not. The chapter head note states that the chapter does not cover edible nuts. It is the chapter on nuts, why does it not cover edible nuts?

What this illustrates is that classifying commodities can be a real challenge. There are interpretations, notes, sub notes, even court decisions that all become a part of the classification challenge. Even with many of the helpful tools, some countries, including the United States, provide (See the United States

37

International Trade Commission lookup tool http://hts.usitc.gov, classification can be a challenge.

As a general proposition, I can offer the following advice when it comes to classification and other regulated activities. *Do your best to document how you came to your conclusion.* Doing your best is not just going through perfunctory motions. Documenting includes ensuring that the person, whether it is you or someone else, who made the determination can demonstrate a diligent effort to learn the process and the applicable rules and who can document what work went into the classification process itself, especially if there is uncertainty surrounding the item.

That might be a file with publication clips or chemical composition study or an expert opinion. In one company I was with we employed a third party chemist to validate our internal classifications. If you do that level diligence you will be in a strong position to defend your determination in the event of audit or inquiry. At one company where I worked, we used an outside chemist to assist in the classification of certain chemical compounds.

Trusted Traders

Importers and exporters who can demonstrate diligence complying with applicable rules are clearly more worthy of trust than traders with a history of penalties and an inability to demonstrate compliance efforts.

In an increasing number of countries, these traders are given a trusted trader designation in recognition of their compliance program because they represent a reduced compliance threat. However, there is another kind of threat, one that is not about fraud.

I introduced earlier the notion of an "unknown" shipper. The unknown shipper is an unfamiliar entity to border officers. Unknown entities represent threats at multiple levels, at the top of which is the possibility of terrorism. The story of the bomb hidden in a printer tendered to UPS is an example. UPS discovered that anomaly. Consequently, carriers are often thought of as the first defense when it comes to terror plots using the commercial transportation system.

There are other threats: contraband to avoid taxes (e.g., cigarettes), narcotics, banned pornography, and smuggled weapons. Carriers, in particular, ocean carriers moving freight containers into which they have no visibility, are not a very good first line of defense. The burden falls on customs officers at ports.

The problem is that most shipments are legitimate, detecting criminal activity becomes a matter of finding the rare dangerous exception amongst a huge volume of container goods. The unpredictable bumps in the road referred to earlier arise from random, and targeted, interdictions during transit.

Security Partnerships

To reduce the size of the threat as much as possible, a concept known as *trusted trader* has arisen. These programs are, rhetorically at least, "public private partnerships." There are variations of this from country to country.

In many countries, the "categorization" falls under the oversight of Authorized Economic Operator ("AEO"). In the European Union, there are three types of AEOs: 1) those with security approvals; 2) those with compliance approvals and 3) those admitted to both security and compliance programs.

http://ec.europa.eu/taxation_customs/customs/policy_issues/customs_security/aeo/index_en.htm

In the United States the analogs are "C-TPAT" (the Customs and Trade Partnership Against Terrorism) and "ISA" (Importer Self-assessment) and most recently, a designation for those who are both. The ISA and European Compliance designations are given to applicants who pass certain commercial compliance tests (e.g., record keeping requirements). The US C-TPAT and European Security AEO designations are granted for adherence to specified physical security programs that the trader can demonstrate have been implemented.

http://www.cbp.gov/border-security/ports-entry/cargo-security/c-tpat-customs-trade-partnership-against-terrorism

Other countries, including China, Brazil, Japan, Australia, Mexico, and others have adopted variations of the AEO convention.

The express purpose of these programs is to reduce the size of the risk threat and avoid the unnecessary obstacles to trade referred to at the outset of this book. As much as governments will argue that they are effective at securing transport with the AEO programs (eliminated trusted trader transit interruptions), I have not seen much evidence of it. As a consequence, many traders, large and small, simply do not apply for admission to AEO programs. There are those that have applied and been admitted that say they see no difference in the frequency of inspections, thus bringing into sharp focus the need to join them. In order to "motivate" more members, countries are withdrawing benefits from companies that do not agree to participate "voluntarily."

Losing trade benefits, such as not having to post bonds to guarantee that duty will paid is a good reason for companies to join those programs and it may be beneficial for the growing SME to explore what economic benefits may accrue. Whether you decide to have your company apply, there is no question that the standards that exist in these programs *are best practices and worth adopting.*

Policies and Procedures to Prevent Trouble

Assuming that you are a "trustworthy" trader, ensuring that the organization is actually adhering to best practices, whether you choose an AEO or not, is a basic requirement for good international business. Evidencing trustworthiness starts with written policies and procedures. If your company does not have written policies and procedures to implement them, you cannot evidence trustworthiness. Nor will the company be able to defend itself in the event of a governmental compliance audit.

SME Inc. made a mistake in a declaration. Instead of declaring a good at $19.00 per unit, the order clerk entered 19 cents, which resulted in an error of several thousand dollars and a substantial underpayment of duty. The customs officer reviewing the document noticed the invoice was too low for the product being shipped. As computers are known to make the same mistake over and over, the officer pulled the last few declarations and found the same mistake. He

40

determined that there was pattern of under declaration of value and; therefore, a lack of adequate controls to assure the proper filing of declarations. The next thing that happened was a visit to the importer. When asked to see records, including accounting records and process controls to assure the accuracy of customs declarations, the trader could not coherently respond. There followed a massively burdensome audit of all of the traders' import records, substantial legal fees and a sizable penalty.

Spot Audits

The need for strong internal controls is certainly not unique to international trade but it is somewhat more perilous to do business without them. Customs authorities do not need warrants to visit any of the company offices and inspect the company files. No other law enforcement authority has that authority. Let's us consider the case of the SME above. What might have been a credible defense?

Earlier, we referred to customs classification uncertainty. The example used was canned peaches. Several different HS classifications might apply, but only one is correct. If one had made such a determination based on diligent research, one would want to show how they arrived at a determination during that spot audit. You will want to provide documentary proof that the classification was not arbitrary.

Similarly, SME Inc. should have had and presented as a defense documented procedures to demonstrate how the company would have discovered the $19 error and what it would have done to correct the error when discovered. For example, "a post entry audit" against other source documents (such as price lists or purchase orders) would have discovered the error and enabled SME to voluntarily disclose it to customs eventually.

Transfer Pricing

Inter-company pricing, otherwise known as "transfer pricing" is the price charged for goods between related entities. Transfer pricing is a particularly problematic pitfall that requires particularly adept documentation to support it. How does one prove that the prices on inter-company invoices obey the rules?

The answer is to have documented evidence of the process followed and the inputs used to derive at a lawful number. That may be a transfer pricing study or an attorney review. Perhaps it is the same price the vendor charges to all buyers as evidenced in published price lists. The point is to have documents that demonstrate real control.

Those readers who are not faced with transfer pricing issues can skip this section. Everyone else is warned that what follows is an invitation to seek professional counsel from experts in the field of international transfer pricing. Companies like Ernst & Young, KPMG, PWC, and other big accounting firms should be consulted and their work product should be included in the corporate archives, documenting the compliance efforts.

Tax Versus Duty

It is a curiosity of trade between related parties that different departments of government with taxing authority have different objectives and have developed different rules regarding valuation that are often at odds with each other.

Consider the company that manufactures in a low-income tax jurisdiction and sells to its affiliate in a higher tax jurisdiction. The buying affiliate then resells the imported product in the domestic market, for example between Singapore and the United States.

The SME wants the export price to be as high as possible in order to keep profits in Singapore, where it pays a lower tax. The Internal Revenue Service of the United States might, therefore, wonder whether that invoice (transfer) price to its affiliate is unduly overstated so that the domestic profit is kept low! US Customs might decide that the invoice is understated in order to pay less duty!

The conflict is that the Internal Revenue wants a low import price (in order to collect more domestic tax) and customs wants a high import price (in order to collect more duty). The problem is one of creating a transfer pricing protocol that satisfies both the Revenue and the Customs and to have files that support that.

Customs Valuation

Transfer pricing is beyond the scope of this book, consult an expert in international transfer pricing. As far as customs valuation is concerned, there is a hierarchy of rules that is used to determine value for customs.

There are six basic methods, starting with Transaction Value, which, as previously mentioned, is the price actually paid or payable between unrelated parties. The six methods are:

Method1 — Transaction value
https://www.wto.org/english/tratop_e/cusval_e/cusval_info_e.htm#a_1

Method2 — Transaction value of identical goods
https://www.wto.org/english/tratop_e/cusval_e/cusval_info_e.htm#a_2

Method3 — Transaction value of similar goods
https://www.wto.org/english/tratop_e/cusval_e/cusval_info_e.htm#a_3

Method4 — Deductive method
https://www.wto.org/english/tratop_e/cusval_e/cusval_info_e.htm#a_4

Method5 — Computed method
https://www.wto.org/english/tratop_e/cusval_e/cusval_info_e.htm#a_5

Method6 — Fall-back method
https://www.wto.org/english/tratop_e/cusval_e/cusval_info_e.htm#a_6

The logic is that if Method 1 is not applicable (because the conditions are not met), Method 2 is attempted. If it does not apply, Method 3 is applied, (Methods 5 and 6 are somewhat interchangeable).

There is a good article explanation of these methods and the conditions that must be met at the World Trade Organization website.

https://www.wto.org/english/tratop_e/cusval_e/cusval_info_e.htm

As with all things international, there are decisions, case law and implementing regulations in the various countries that might apply to a specific industry. If there is doubt, consult an expert.

Whichever method is used, the paramount rule I have stressed is document, document, and document; write, distribute, and audit compliance with company policies and have a trained company representative ready to answer questions should the need arise.

Part IV - Getting Paid

Logistics is the last link before the goods are transported into the vast trade lanes. Logistics is a critical part of the process of getting-paid.

When I worked at Warner Lambert, a position was created called "asset management," which was responsible for inventory and receivables. That may seem like an odd pairing, but accounts receivables, is the money owed to the company from trapped cash, like inventory.

Growing a global business requires a thought process that money owed should be managed as tightly as inventory and that includes recognizing that selling internationally creates challenges not encountered when selling domestically. These challenges are in two broad categories: physical risks and financial risks.

Loss and Damage Risk

Physical challenges are those mostly beyond the control of both the seller and the buyer. Those include delays at borders as indicated in the parts of this book on *border bumps*. Goods sitting in customs-detained facilities are targets for theft and exposure to damaging elements. In some ports, customs compounds are uncovered and exposed to rain and heat.

Physical risks related to theft or damage are a constant threat and they increase as distances and time elapsed increase and with the attractiveness of the commodity to organized crime. Easily "fenced" (sold) consumer goods are at much higher risk of theft than bulk chemicals. It is helpful to leave identifying markings off packaging so as not to reveal information about the consignee (customer) or the contents. The customer's broker, destination port, an order number and the number of packages are really all that are needed. Periodically, changing the marking will help to disguise the nature of the parties and the contents.

If the company has sufficient volume to ship by sea freight in containers, that is the best protection. Otherwise, shrouded pallets with heavy banding is an option. If that is still too much, over-packing in master cartons is a must for all consumer products.

Credit Risk

Selling internationally is not like selling in the local market. Your customer may be thousands of miles away, speak a different language, and be in an entirely different time zone. It is not likely that you are going to fly over to collect a debt. Indeed, debt collection can be a perilous issue. Law suits in foreign courts are probably not an option in most cases.

Still, from the buyer's point of view, paying in advance is highly undesirable, especially in new relationships. You may be late shipping or not ship at all. The product may not be up to specification or arrive damaged and unusable. Thus, extension of payment "terms" is a marketing necessity in most cases. (As indicated earlier, cash buyers should be considered warily.)

Similarly, receiving terms from vendors for purchases is a necessary part of doing business whether buying raw materials or for retail sale. Just as managing cash trapped in inventory is important to a successful global startup, so is the management of receivables. This has two aspects: assurance of getting paid and assurance of adequate cash flow to finance operations. If the company cannot meet payroll or buy additional raw materials because the business is owed money, it may go bankrupt.

Collection Instruments

Selling internationally increases the risks associated with receivables. There are various ways to minimize this risk, including the use of international documentary letters of credit. These instruments substitute the credit risk associated with the customer or country for the bank's own creditworthiness. The process is that the buyer goes to a bank in its country and requests a line of credit. The bank in the importer's country is familiar with the buyer and is able to assure that it gets paid. The "originating" bank then notifies its correspondent bank, usually in major trading centers, that a letter of credit has been opened in the company name as the beneficiary.

The company is guaranteed payment if it complies with the terms, including shipping within the expiration of the LC. When the shipment is made and proof of shipment is presented, the originating bank authorizes the correspondent bank to pay your company on presentation of shipment documents, typically bills of lading, invoices, and packing lists. Terms can still be extended using the LC, but it is the bank, not the seller, that promises to make payment according to the terms. The bank substitutes its credit worthiness for that of the buyer.

Letters of Credit are a good way to assure payment, but they are not free, they tie up the buyer's credit lines, and exporters very frequently fail to comply with terms and then left without protection and extended payment delays.

It is possible to ship goods but to deny the importer access to the documents needed to pick up the cargo by sending the controlling documents to a bank for collection. When the buyer pays the "draft," it is given the documents and can pick up the goods. If the buyer decides not to go through with the transaction, the seller must retrieve goods that may be located across the world.

Clearly, there is a certain amount of trust involved in selling goods in this way, the question is "if you trust the customer why not sell on an open account basis?" This presents the least of all protections but if the client is trustworthy ("know your customer"), it may work. In recent years, payments using "Bitcoin" technology have begun to emerge. The payment mechanism is made by redeeming electronic credits emailed by the buyer to the seller. This form of payment is still very much in its infancy and has risk of volatile currency fluctuations.

It may be preferable, for an SME to discount the receivable when payment terms, such as 60 days, have been extended by selling the receivable. Commercial paper is considered a safe tool and used to finance international trade in many parts of the world. "Factors" will pay your invoice, less a discount, and wait to get paid. There are many ways of getting paid, all associated with more or less risk.

The SME is well advised to become acquainted with the methods available for collecting payment and with them, the many options, each appropriate for particular types of business. Major trading centers, such as New York, London, and Hong Kong are important centers of trade finance.

Exchange Risk

Another risk to be considered is fluctuation in exchange rates. This is particularly relevant in long-lived and high-value contracts, such as providing construction supplies or services. The buying power of a currency will go up or down every day and over a long period the change can be substantial enough to make a profitable arrangement a loser and a marginal arrangement profitable.

Most trade is conducted in US dollars. If you are an American importer and you buy goods in Italy in dollars, fluctuations in the value of the Euro will not affect your profitability on any given transaction. If you are Italian selling your goods in Euros, a decrease in the value of the Euro will increase your cost of goods.

Over time, the American importer will see a price rise for the same good if the Euro falls in relation to the dollar because the Italian will buy less. Similarly, all things being equal, an American who is selling goods to Italy will sell more when the dollar is weak against the Euro.

Most export and import trade continues to be conducted using the US dollar as the exchange medium. For all fluctuations, the dollar continues to be the most attractive currency for international trade.

Impact of Exchange on Foreign Expansion

The impact of currency fluctuations are challenging to manage when a business expands outside of its economic boundaries. For example, a French company that builds a factory in Ohio or an American company expanding into Ireland will invest substantial dollars (or Euro) in a different monetary market.

Long-lived exchange swings will be reflected in how much money is left after expenses when that number is translated back to the parent country currency. We often see news reports of multinational companies reporting lower profits attributable to exchange fluctuations even though sales in the other market remain strong.

Global Sourcing

While we are on the subject of money, as the small buyer of a less-well-known company, your larger supplier may have qualms about your company's creditworthiness. In the section on getting paid, we addressed documentary letters or credit to substitute your customer's credit for yours.

Obviously, if you are the buyer, the same method is available for your purchases. Your bank establishes a line of credit for you and guarantees payment to the supplier upon presentation of documents, evidencing that a shipment has occurred and is not irretrievable (for practical purposes) so are you guaranteed to get the merchandise.

Opening a letter of credit is a great tool if your supplier questions your ability to pay. What if you need funds to buy the raw materials to manufacture goods for which you have a customer? This was the case in Greece during the Euro crisis. In such a case, you may employ a "back-to-back" letter of credit. A back-to-back letter of credit. The first LC the buyer opens in your name, then you use an LC as collateral for the LC on the supplier, the supplier ships the goods, the documents are presented, then the bank pays the supplier, you manufacture goods, ship, present documents and the bank pays you.

A back-to-back letter of credit is used to assure your suppliers payment for manufacturing inputs. Let us say you have the possibility of a large order for Christmas perfume and watch kits from Marks & Spencer. You are going to manufacture the fragrance but need to source the watches. It is a large volume and you are a "not too well known" SME in Spain. The Swiss watch seller needs "cash in advance," which you do not have or a confirmed and irrevocable letter of credit. You do not have the assets to secure a letter of credit on your own. What do you do?

You convince Marks & Spencer that you will deliver but need a back-to-back LC. The buyer is getting a good deal and knows it. It opens an LC in your name, which is confirmed by a prime Swiss bank and is payable 60 days after presentation of shipping documents from the Swiss watchmaker. You use that instrument to open an LC on the watchmaker. The watchmaker ships goods and is paid. You now have 60 days to assemble the kit and ship to Marks &

Spencer. When you go and present the shipping documents, the Swiss watchmaker and you are paid.

The previous example gives you a good idea of how a back-to-back LC might be used to enable a manufacturing SME to sell against an internally financed large company.

Versatile Letters of Credit

Alternatively, it may be that you are a manufacturer's representative and want an LC to assure that you get paid your legitimate sales commission when your supplier ships. The supplier does not trust that you are going to get paid and then pay it and wants an LC to name it as the beneficiary, not you. In such a case, a confirmed and irrevocable LC can be opened in the name of the supplier as beneficiary with a portion of the proceeds going to you. When shipment is made, you both get paid.

Another form of LC is the standby letter of credit. In this case, the supplier is not insisting on a letter of credit to consummate the transaction but wants a guarantee that it will be paid if the buyer fails to live up to its commitment. In the kiting example above, the Swiss watchmaker may have asked for a standby letter of credit. If payment is to be made by a certain date and the buyer (the Spanish company) does not present documents, the Swiss company can demand payment under the standby credit.

All of these instruments are subject to expiration. It can be expiration for payment, or expiration for shipment (with a later payment date), or both.

They are either confirmed or unconfirmed and revocable or irrevocable. Revocability is what is says, it can be revoked by the customer at any time. Confirmation is another matter. A Letter of Credit is opened by a bank, typically the customer's bank in his country, for example, the Bank of Littleville. The buyer in Thailand does not know that bank and does not have any more faith in it than in the seller so it requires the LC to be confirmed by a major international bank such as JP Morgan Chase. The Bank of Littleville opens the Letter of Credit and JP Morgan Chase confirms it in Bangkok.

All Letters of Credit are "documentary" because they are all about documents. The minimum required documentation is an invoice (here it is again) and proof of shipment such as a bill of lading or airway bill evidencing shipment of the good. Notice that unlike the nomenclature used for customs clearance, the words used in the commercial invoice for the bank must be the trade nomenclature used between the buyer and the seller. So the commercial invoice reads "Hawaiian specials" while the customs declaration reads "desiccated coconut". Notably, the bill of lading may read "packaged foodstuffs," which might cause a problem.

I prepared or checked documents under letters of credit for a long time as a foreign freight forwarder. There are a few truths that remain to this day. Bank checkers are the people who examine documents and then authorize payment. They deal in documents not merchandise and look for the same text in negotiable documents as it appears in the LC. No exemptions. Deviations will result in a finding of discrepancy and the assurance of the LC is voided.

There were many times, when as a forwarder I read certain difficult to comply with terms in an LC, I concluded that they buyer had inserted terms the seller could not comply with in order to void the protections of the letter of credit. As freight forwarder my role was to arrange shipment exactly as specified including preparing and presenting documents to the negotiating back according to the expiration date. Many times the "required for shipment date" could not be met. These invariably resulted in protracted payment delays.

The lesson learned is when a letter of credit is received it must be reviewed line by line to assure every requirement can be met. That not only includes meeting compulsory dates but complying every other detail as well. If your company name is not exactly as it appears in the letter of credit, it has to be amended. If the product name is spelled incorrectly in the LC you have two choices. Use the same spelling in your commercial invoice or request an amendment. If the shipping or negotiation dates cannot be met, get an extension. If you are asked to do something illegal or contrary to policy, reject it.

Part V - Supply Chain Networks

At some point, SME unit volume for export or import or both becomes significant enough that the company will start thinking about expanding physical presence beyond its domestic boundaries. That may consist of a first factory overseas, a new contract manufacturing agreement, or one or more service or distribution centers.

Or perhaps the company sees opportunities in dealing directly with suppliers located outside of the country instead of working through domestic manufacturer's representatives that appear to add no value but which do add cost.

Over time, the benefits of "globalization" become more apparent and attainable. You see benefit being closer to your markets, to your suppliers. The world is a big place. Your business should have no constraining boundaries and theoretically it doesn't.

As that happens, the need to focus sharply on basic strategies becomes even more important because the complexities of global networks are another level of complication. There is an increasing need to see the business in both global and local terms.

Basic Strategy

Whatever your business, you will want to assure that your high-level strategic goals are met. You want to be sure your expansion plans

Are sustainable to satisfy your commitment to your customers

You will need to consistently and reliably deliver product to the markets in which you reside according to your service promise. If your promise is 24-hour delivery to a home in Tibet, can you consistently deliver?

Support your market pricing and cost strategy

If you must have a way to deliver directly to homes in Tibet, can you pay the freight, duty and taxes and still make a profit?

Comply with regulations on both the export and import side

Are the regulations applicable to the business and market going to frustrate your service commitments? For example, is the time to get an export license predictable? Will the agriculture regulators promptly conduct inspections?

Continually monitor evolving patterns and adjust accordingly

Do you have a way to consistently monitor development in the market that can impact our business? For example, how will you learn a competitor is opening for business next door? Are trade disputes likely in the commodities with which you are involved? Are the laws regulating your commodity changing?

Provide access to expert services we might need when we need them

Do we know who to go to for expert services? The decision about location will take into account many factors, including but not limited to:

- Economic incentives by the local government

- Taxes

- Labor considerations

- Facility costs (cost of ownership)

- Utility costs

- Communications

- Regulatory environment

- Political stability

- Rule of law

- Corruption

- Logistics

The logistics of a second, third, or more locations, (i.e. service centers), will, in turn, take into account a variety of factors that we will explore at a high level. Those can be broken down into two broad categories: *inbound and outbound*.

Inbound considerations are an assessment of the costs and feasibility of receiving goods for manufacturing or inventory. Does adequate transportation exist? Is it competitive? For example, if goods are delivered to the service center by railroad, is there only one track? Are you a "hostage" to one carrier? As discussed earlier, under *concepts of transportation*, availability of competitive transportation is a strategic imperative.

Adequate inbound transportation is true whether you are going global or remaining within your home country. The added complication of an international location is that you will be crossing borders. Here, the existence of trade programs becomes a relevant issue.

First assume that you are not considering a volatile location, by which I include places torn by war or civil disobedience and which are not subject to governmental sanctions, either by your parent country or that of important customers.

From the universe of remaining possible locations, it is important to consider whether the commodity you will be importing for manufacturing or retail is subject to arbitrary, confusing, or unpredictable government regulations.

Medicines are an example. In some jurisdictions, the mere appearance of violation can frustrate a shipment without a rule on how the regulator has to resolve the issue. That is unpredictable and can put a company out of business unexpectedly. "Appearance" to one person may not be apparent to another. That adds the additional uncertainty that the border hurdle is arbitrary.

If the products being imported or exported are subject to this brand of regulation, it is important to determine in advance with the assistance of experts in the specific market what the regulatory landscape is like before making an investment.

On the outbound side the primary consideration is the availability of dependable transportation to your markets at competitive rates. To the extent you are in a "back haul" location, you may have an advantage. In any case, you must know that transportation costs are sustainable.

Managing the Supply Chain

Once you have established a market or goal to do so, and marketing, legal, tax, facility, and people issues have been addressed; and the investment has been set aside, attention turns, in more detail, to the next crucial executable—the supply chain. All of those other factors aside, the supply chain must work at the locations you have in mind. More specifically, does the location assure that you can:

1. Meet your service commitments to your customers? This means delivering product in good condition within the time frame promised. This is true whether the customer is internal or external.

2. Achieve your profit objectives? Will you consistently hit your assumed <u>landed cost targets</u> established in planning? Landed means inclusive of logistical, duty, tax, and administrative costs.

3. Assure a sustainable business? Are you absolutely a good corporate citizen wherever you do business, observing the applicable laws as well as the social norms expected of modern businesses, e.g., green and fair labor policies?

4. Enable growth? Does that location enable long-term growth or is it severely limited to the one country and its fortunes?

You must allow sufficient breathing room to seed new markets with adapted products, policies, and logistical capabilities. Fundamental to all of this is a capability to meet demand as the business grows without short-changing existing customers.

How Easy Is it to do Business in a Country?

A prime consideration in deciding where to do business, especially international business, is how hard or easy it is to do business in a particular country. Part of that is how difficult it is to get in or out if you are considering sourcing from it.

The World Bank attempts to quantify how easy or difficult logistics are in different countries in an index that captures several factors, including customs. The best performing country of 2014 is Germany. The worst performing country is Somalia. The United States ranks 9th on the list. If you are considering a facility, it is advisable to take a look at the World Bank's ranking as a factor in deciding where to do business.

http://lpi.worldbank.org/international/global

Once you have made your site location decision based on the variety of factors, and others appropriate for your business, you will need to consider service partners because accomplishing those goals is going to require strong partners as well as marketing partners.

You will want to determine which Logistics Service Providers appear best positioned to achieve your specific goals (e.g., expertise in the market) and then sit with them to discuss your plan, what costs are assumed under different scenarios (e.g., same-day, next-day delivery commitment), what bumps other clients have faced in the target markets, and how they have managed them.

In the case of warehouses, you will want to assure that they meet the sanitary and safety requirements of your product and are situated conveniently to the geographic locations that you are interested in reaching. It certainly a plus if similar products in the same warehouse, albeit not necessarily competitors.

Since all logistical planning is a function of volume, an essential part of the discussion is forecasting volume, including frequency, shipment sizes, and anticipated order cycle times.

The importance of physically visiting facilities cannot be overestimated. I recall the case of a very large toy manufacturer that closed its own warehouses as a cost cutting measure and engaged a large logistics service provider to manage all its European distribution. On paper and in sales presentations the LSP was ideal. The manufacturer never visited the LSP facility itself. As its own warehouses shut down and volume through the LSP increased it became apparent that the problems being encountered with the LSP were not merely start-up hiccups. The facility was inadequate. It was too small and configured inappropriately for the kind of handling the manufacturer required.

Visiting proposed facilities, be they warehouses or contract manufacturers or even trucking terminals, periodically and unannounced, is a best practice. When I was hired as traffic manager at Parke-Davis, a drug company located in

Detroit, I visited the terminal of its New York City area trucker. It was dirty, insecure and no other drugs were being handled. The rates were certainly low but good distribution practices trumped and I switched truckers. I am certain, my predecessor would not have worked with that trucker if he had ever visited the terminal.

Forecasting the Volume

Entering new domestic markets, adding product lines to existing markets, and creating significant new demand all have logistical consequences that need to be "forecasted." Three dimensions of this are:

1. Increased volume measured in both units sold (hence shipment size) and number of transactions (frequency)

2. Growth in stock keeping units—that is to say variations of the basic product

3. Growth in capital requirements—in logistics terms that focus on the ability to pay suppliers

Adding international business can create additional challenges of its own. One is a new tension between servicing existing domestic customers (the ones who pay the rent) and new foreign customers that may possibly represent the future

An SME can try to satisfy the requirements of one, the other, or both. But failing to balance the allocation of resources to each will certainly result in lost business opportunity and possibly even failure of the business.

The incremental international business may be significantly more involved than simply adding another thousand units to the manufacturing plan and more challenging than merely adding an overtime shift. For example, will you need a different formulation for the new market? Will the packaging be different? Will the labeling be unique? If you are going into three new markets, will you need three new labels? What will this mean in terms of machine down time?

It is generally accepted than anything can happen to make a forecast unreliable. The best forecast is one based on as many facts as possible. You can always look back and see where you made errors, but the mistake will not be your last.

Thus, depending on your industry, it is probably better to fill too many cans of your product with safety stock than too few. Safety stock is cash that has been trapped in raw materials, work in progress, and finished goods that have not been sold. To stay in business, the SME needs to have free cash as quickly as possible. In this sense, safety inventory sounds like a bad practice, but failing to satisfy your service commitments will quickly deplete cash, because it will not be coming in.

Logistically, whether your business model is *made to order* or *to forecast,* you will need to decide what Logistics Service Provider will handle raw materials and components, where they will be stored, and how quickly they will need to be delivered to go into production. (There is more on this in the section on duty management strategies.)

Manufacturing companies that go from plants in one country to two or more countries for manufacture do so either by acquisition or building brick and mortar businesses. In my experience, each presents unique issues as well as common opportunities to leverage existing capabilities. Acquiring an existing company with multiple locations presents yet other challenges for both the acquiring and the acquired company.

Acquisitions

I have worked at both acquiring and acquired companies. The technical challenges in both scenarios are secondary to the issues arising from the people involved. Managers and employees on both sides often feel that their way is the better way and that the newcomer is just plain wrong. This is especially true in the acquired company, in which there is fear of loss of job or demotion. The focus shifts from substance to personalities and the business suffers.

In divestitures, I have seen managers in the divesting company "dump" low performers into the organization being divested. I have seen really inept people placed in senior positions in the new organization. I recall one case where a manager who was to be terminated was placed as the senior functional leader in the receiving organization.

The problem is if you are the acquiring a company, you do not know the folks in the acquired business. You do not know who is going to contribute or who is going to be a drag on the business and you cannot determine who would be better at a particular function, the person in your organization or the incumbent in the other.

Those matters are complicated by cultural, language, and ethnic differences in international expansion. I have seen women do extraordinarily well in environments where women are treated as essential to the operation. Those same women did not flourish in countries where women were not expected to be part of the decision apparatus. In one case that I recall, the woman rose to become the office leader and boss to the former unit executive and she did a much better job than he had.

The challenge for the CEO in relationships such as these that bring together multiple operations is to objectively determine what is best for the combined operation. I am not aware of any guaranteed organizational change process to accomplish this, especially in international business.

It might seem as though objective, quasi-scientific tools, can be used. Perhaps that is true to some extent, but the inherent bias of the manager making that assessment can prejudice the outcome. I recall a case in which the acquired company had in place a superior order processing system to the acquiring company. The better system was removed in favor of the antiquated one. There was rational explanation; there always is, the unanswerable question is *was the decision objective*?

I have been in a case where the opposite was true. The acquiring company CEO believed that everything about the target was better than what he had. When the deal consummated and the operations came together, the parent company operation was eviscerated. In the end, the two businesses were fundamentally different! Each was the way it was because of the market it was in, not because one complement was better or smarter than the other.

Transportation

There are only so many liner ocean carriers in the world. (A *liner* operator is an ocean carrier with regularly scheduled sailings offered to the general public, as opposed to a charter operator). It cannot hurt to speak with the sales representative in the larger affiliate about leveraging the global business. It may be possible to sign global service contracts in the major markets. That really does not work with airlines. Unless the company is a very large shipper, most airlines prefer to deal with air freight forwarders.

Service providers

If you are working with globalized freight forwarding companies, it may pay to have a global service discussion. The larger air freight forwarders and non-vessel-operating (ocean) common carriers have offices or agents throughout the world. They are needed to "de-consolidate" consolidated shipments and to sell to inbound services to importers. To the extent that freight is paid in a common currency (dollars), it is possible to have global discussions.

The most contentious internal disagreements I have ever experienced had to do with trying to force global contracts on local operations. There are lots of reasons for this: 1) the local affiliate knows the local environment and headquarters does not; 2) service tends to be great in one region but terrible in another; 3) the global contract lowers overall company costs but increases local costs.

Those are all legitimate arguments that have to be weighed carefully, but there are the less-valid but nonetheless challenging issues that make consensus building difficult. Among those are the personal relationships at the center of the company-service provider relation. Personal relationships cannot be measured in dollars. They cannot be measured at all, but they may be critical to success or failure. In those cases, unless local logistics are critical to the acquisition or integration for some reason (such as the desire for a global tracking capability), it is best to postpone the decision until more is understood about the organization.

Computer systems

There is the question *can we leverage the existing system* – viz. order processing, invoicing, AR/AP, warehouse, inventory, supply chains, forecasting etcetera?

Typically, those are separate modules and that may or may not be integrated into the corporate Enterprise Resource Planning (ERP) system. If you are looking to integrate multiple systems internationally, the host of issues raised are multiple and difficult. Basic issues such as "are the product field lengths the same" or "are the raw material component numbers harmonized for the same component across applications?"

I have been involved in several situations where the product ID used by the ordering location is different from the product ID used by the supplying location and different still from the product ID used by the major customer!

It is my view that the <u>concept</u> of enterprise integration can be more elegant than the reality. The management question is *how much integration is needed, what will it cost, and what will the level of angst be?* Then, double the dollar estimate and triple the time.

Export\Import Systems

As the number of customers, markets, supply points, product variations and transaction volume increase, the possibility of getting export documents and import declarations consistently accurate becomes exponentially more difficult. There are different languages involved, multiple price structures and terms, special clauses, unique customer, instructions and so on.

Robust systems are needed very early in the internationalization process. You probably already have installed, either the acquired or acquiring company, some level of trade automation and the question is can or should you try to leverage these and why?

There may well be core functionality that may make it possible to install at multiple international locations and that would be great. But do not assume full functionality to be transplantable. For example, as we discussed, the HS number is universal to the first six digits. The customs harmonized number should be useful across the organization.

Aside from strictly "customs" oriented functionality, the other question that comes up is *how much and* what *do I integrate to the corporate environment?* For example, having a global view of inventories, demand, and manufacturing capability is a good thing, especially if there are many line items to keep track of at multiple locations.

In a global business, you want to be able to route input materials where they are needed and to whatever extent possible move manufacturing from one location to another as needed. That is particularly useful where there are multiple steps to manufacturing and inventory at every step. To the extent that the final step can be postponed until product is pulled by the market, there is flexibility in moving materials and minimizing inventory. You cannot do this without global visibility. If you can do it with spreadsheets, that is great but at some point, Excel spreadsheets stop being feasible.

Networks

As the organization grows and the number of markets, suppliers, and factories grows, the logistical network becomes increasingly complex in every aspect and the need for visibility across the organization grows.

Understanding the network graphically through simple drawings helps to conceptualize planning. Where should my principal and secondary repositories of finished and semi-finished goods, spare parts, raw materials, and packaging components be?

The more complex the organization, the more challenging it becomes to optimize the operation. *Is it time to think about global procurement contracts? Should I inventory in country X for markets ABC? Does that make logistical sense?*

Software that draws pictures such as this and can redraw the pictures "on demand" can be extremely useful, especially if the data needed to generate the picture can be captured electronically. Your systems should do more than process transactions. They should be a source of intelligence as well.

Drawing the network enables visualization of options. The arrows and shapes in the picture representing factories, distribution centers and markets can be adjusted in relative size to a pinpoint service issues, market size and transportation spend. Locations ideally suited to function as logistical centers for finished and/or manufacturing inputs can be more easily planned as well.

Models such as this can be used to indicate duty and even tax exposure under various assumptions. For example, what if I source from A instead of B to take advantage of a trade agreement? Factories A, B, and C are all in different countries serving market D. Sourcing market D through B is the lesser cost option. It's the sum of costs between A, B, and D compared with A, C, and D.

The numbers can refer to anything—capacity, taxes, cost of goods, transportation, days inventory needed. Planning the optimal network starts to answer questions that otherwise would be resolved based on personalities and opinions and not objectively.

For example, the forwarder in Amsterdam is terrific but we have decided to source North America from Japan and those services are no longer needed. Or in negotiation with an air freight forwarder, it can be demonstrated that to keep the business, the costs from C to D have to be lower than B to D.

Software to calculate optimization and draw those graphics are readily available. The key is having data that are accurate and economical to harvest to enable analysis on a recurring basis as conditions and the metrics themselves change.

Compliance

An important resource that can and should be leveraged throughout the growing organization is a corporate compliance program. Procedures may, by necessity, be local because uniquely titled positions and/or specifically named people may be assigned that are going to be different from location to location. For example, the corporate policy might (should be): "A copy of every customs entry must be maintained and available for inspection at any time in accordance with local regulatory requirements".

In Country A, the implementing procedure might say:

The Import Manager shall maintain a hardcopy file of every customs declaration...

The implementation of the policy in Country B might say:

The Procurement manger shall maintain a hardcopy file of all customs declaration...

Both of those implementing procedures comply with the corporate policy and are flexible to accommodate local practices. What is important is that there are corporate policies that demonstrate the corporation's commitment to regulatory compliance and that they must be backed by local audit-able procedures.

In some companies, third parties are engaged to conduct audits. Some companies engage consultants, others lawyers, and others accounting type firms. Other companies assign this task to a corporate function, such as Internal Audit and others, the larger ones, create a position or department to conduct post entry audits and otherwise ensure compliance with corporate policies and local regulations. What is important is that when the regulator visits, the company has the documents and files that demonstrate that they are diligent in seeking to assure corporate compliance.

Please note that even highly compliant companies are going to make mistakes. The role of senior management is to assure the organization has implemented auditable processes and procedures designed to discover and correct those errors or omissions.

Export Customer Service

On the sales side, not enough has been said of the need to parallel grow customer service capabilities as transaction volume increases, new markets are entered and products diversity. The more products and variations (SKU) you add to your catalog, the more complex the "order taking" task becomes. Given differences in language, cultural norms and other factors, the more markets (countries) you sell to the more complex the order-taking process. This vital front end function is basic to customer service and growing your international business.

Increasingly, buyers, especially consumers, are relying on the Internet to view catalogs and place orders. Unless the catalog is very dense or the product is very simple, at some point in the pre or post buy cycle the customer will want to speak with a customer service representative. Nothing is more destructive to successful growth than a person representing the company who does not know the product. Add to that the complexity of export-import trade and the need for experienced, hopefully multilingual or multicultural customer service representatives.

Before allowing an employee to answer the phone, be sure you would want to speak with that person yourself if you were a customer.

In many cases, businesses are just not suitable for online marketing due to the complexity or customization requirements of the product. In those cases, training customer service representatives is as critical as training quality assurance specialists. Every SME should ask itself "are our customer service representatives deeply familiar with our products? Our company? Are they trained on export-import processes?

Whether sales are primarily taken by phone or electronically, a growing business needs systems that are capable of handling increased volume efficiently. Internationally, your system may need to be capable of

1. Foreign language script (headings and content)

2. Inclusion of special text (customs declarations and notes)

3. Additions to the product invoice amount (for example, freight)

4. Differentiated pricing (different prices by customer and country)

5. Printing regulatory information (such as harmonized numbers)

6. Provide for generation of packing lists and other documents

Whether accomplished electronically or otherwise, export systems must assure that denied parties, sanctioned countries, and products requiring a license or permit are captured at order entry and before shipment (see section on regulatory issues).

The importance of at least some automation on the front end as the business grows cannot be overstated. Whether that means enabling a customer service representative to scan a catalog of a thousand parts, while the overseas customer is on hold, to find the perfect fit, or whether it means that orders will enter through Web interfaces or is received electronically through electronic data interfaces (EDI), the growing business must plan and implement systems that will consistently and accurately place demand, track fulfillment, invoice the buyer, and monitor payment. Failing to do this is a certain pathway to failure.

Sales & Operations Planning

Writing the plan is not a late-night, individual undertaking. It is an interactive process involving the people with responsibility for the various supply chain functions. In larger SMEs, sales and marketing people working together with manufacturing, procurement, and finance develop the plan and periodically review actual performance against forecasted activity.

The main purpose of these reviews is to continually adjust the plan according to new information. Metrics form the foundation for assessing the performance of people responsible for sales and marketing, production and logistics and to assure that adequate capital is available to the company to finance operations. Unless these different disciplines are engaged, the process will fail.

Logistically, introduction of new lanes of traffic without planning is a great way to assure competitive pricing and service is not realized.

Border Uncertainty

It is useful at this point to revisit import processes at borders. They are somewhat unpredictable. For many years, one company I worked for imported the same product day after day from the same supplier through the same port of entry. Yet the clearance time was random. Some days, shipments cleared within hours while others took days. Same product, same origin. The level of unpredictability for a given product at a given border varies from country to country and even within countries from border to border.

A number of factors contribute to border unpredictability. How regulated is the commodity? For example, agricultural products present a risk to domestic farmers from the introduction of foreign parasites. Medicines present health risks. Clothing may be subject to quotas created to protect domestic garment interests. The country from which the shipment is made may be on a watch list for terrorism or for political reasons. Knowing what potential obstacles your product may encounter will help you to anticipate and plan defensively.

For example, as covered earlier, an important delaying factor is the importing country's familiarity with the importer and even the exporter. Are you "known" or are you "unknown." Unknown entities are those that have not imported before or import very rarely. These are naturally subject to greater scrutiny because they represent both contraband and terror risks. Hence there is a greater probability of delay.

Other quirks that contribute to flow interruptions include a) the compliance officer is having a bad day; b) there is a seasonal increase in activity at the border crossing with resulting congestion; c) there is a new border control officer; d) there is a typo on a document. I recall a period where experienced officers (that had been hired about the same time) decided to retire at about the same time. The new officers had less than a month training on the job with predictably chaotic results.

As discussed at the outset of this book in some countries, a small facilitation bride is expected to smooth the clearance process and if not paid, papers fall to the bottom of the pile, unnecessarily delaying transit. Major companies (should) refuse to pay these little bribes with the result resolving unpredictability becomes difficult. Complaining to port officials is rarely a good tactic that I have known to backfire. So planning for a longer than average time to clear goods is the best practice where border corruption is known to be a problem.

The relevant point is that a reorder point exists that assures that manufacturing lines or retail shelves will not be exhausted either because of forecast errors or because it took longer to clear inbound goods than expected. Monitoring and recording clearance times will enable realistic minimum\maximum expectations for planning purposes and appropriate investment in safety stock.

I recall a case where I asked a planner how long he provided for customs clearance at a particular port for a particular commodity. Two days, he said. When asked where that number came up he said he assumed it. He was wrong. Historical data indicated the average was closer to five days for clearance and as long as thirty-three!

Supplier Management—A Must

If you are buying finished oods for importation and sale or for parts for internal consumption or manufacturing, developing a strong supplier management program is a must. Pricing may be your procurement manager's starting point and you may base his or her bonus on cost, but that should only be the start.

Common Vision

A common vision with suppliers should include a thorough understanding of where each of you fits into the overall business model of the other. By supplier I include both goods suppliers and service providers.

Whether you are a large company or a small one, consistent, predictable service according to the agreed upon cost and quality model is not negotiable. If you are a "fill-in" for manufacturing slack, when the vendor's large customer has a surge in demand, you will be out of business.

Thought should be given to how to make sure that you are aligned. The incentive or penalty approach may be a good way -reward for exceeded expectations (e.g., reducing the cost of goods) and penalizing for performance failures (e.g., deduction for late delivery).

Common vision should not be unrealistic. A common vision (call it the contract) should be documented and should include all of the critical elements of the relationship. That is true of all supplier relationships but it is especially true of global. For example, admission to AEO or C-TPAT (see security partnerships above) require the importer to assure that the supplier has implemented minimum security procedures. You do not want your container of holiday ornaments to be the vehicle to deliver weapons of mass destruction.

Continuous Vigilance

Having reduced your common expectations to a well-written document, it is critical to continually monitor performance under the agreement. At the top of that list are 1) quality consistency; 2) delivery consistency; 3) social responsibility consistency.

Continually checking quality is self-evident but when you check quality may not be. In some industries, checking your supplier's quality program and supplier's supplier is strongly advised. For example, lead-tainted paint used on toy trucks goes back to the toy maker's supplier. Adulterated animal-based compounds going into pharmaceuticals will show up in the autopsy. Airplanes built with counterfeit brakes might wind up parking in the terminal washroom. Thus, your quality "system" cannot wait for the imported material to be stocked on the store shelf or the manufacturing line.

Social Responsibility

Having established that price is but one element of a sustainable relationship, and that quality is another; let me propose that disassociating your growing business from sweatshops, environmental bandits, and sanctioned sources are high on the priority list.

It is not enough to buy goods of questionable origin at a manufacturer's showroom on 33rd Street in New York City. No one wants to do business with a supplier who uses child labor to sew bikinis. No one wants to eat shark fin soup made from animals thrown back into the sea to drown or use chemicals from plants that dump toxic waste into pristine rivers. Monitoring means <u>physically</u> checking yourself or engaging a private firm to inspect and periodically recheck that supplier offering the great deal. This is basic particularly if you are selling goods to consumers or to socially conscious major corporations, many of which report their social responsibility and "green" initiatives in their public annual reports.

When to Automate

When a business is growing, it may have multiple off-shore suppliers and a more than a dozen export customers. The impact is clerks are working a lot of overtime and there are a lot of clerical errors. There are too many rules to follow, clauses to use on documents, too many different prices due to differentiated strategies based on volume, mix, and market. Spreadsheets are not sufficient any longer.

The available software and how much to spend is beyond the scope of this book. However, there are some thoughts that I can share, such as when and why to invest serious funds in automation.

1. You have many partners (customers, suppliers, LSPs) with special requirements that cannot be left to yellow stickies

2. You have a very regulated business requiring special documentation, record-keeping, permits, or licenses

3. You have a high volume of transactions or transaction lines

4. You have a very short turnaround commitment as in, for example, an Internet-facing customer interface

5. It is taking too long to manually scan for denied parties or sanctions

6. You need to produce documents in multiple languages

7. You are spending a lot on overtime pay

8. You are getting many customer complaints about errors in pricing or failing to observe service requests

9. Your logistics providers are calling about missing, contradictory, or erroneous information or documents

10. You cannot figure out whether you are making or losing money

Another consideration is if the company should attempt to write its own programming code to augment an existing system; write a global application that will integrate the global empire; should the company buy ERP add-ons. The answers to those questions depend on many factors but two main considerations should be:

1. Can you sustain your business without systems to support it?

2. Do you have the internal expertise in trade and IT to build or buy and integrate to your existing systems?

Once those two are settled, it makes sense to ensure that IT does not cost more than it contributes to the bottom line and that it does not consume all the resources in the organization so that focus on the customer is lost.

Import Operations

Depending on how diverse the company import portfolio is, it may be using dozens or even hundreds of different harmonized numbers (see above). You may be dealing with quotas or special programs that reduce your duty exposure and you want to keep track of your supplier performance and payables. There is a lot of money at stake and the potential for fines and penalties is great. When the business has reached this level of dynamism it is time to look at some level of automation.

Consolidating Freight Inbound

Retailers and manufacturers, that "kit" or assemble in a country, will buy from many vendors in a particular region or even a country, e.g., China and bring the goods into a single facility to put them into kits sold as a unity. Often consolidating purchases from various vendors at a central place into full container loads can be a good way to exercise greater control over the logistics and to reduce the cost of transportation.

One way to do this is to engage a forwarder or non-vessel-operating-common-carrier (NVO—a consolidator of freight) at a strategic port of exit in the overseas region (e.g., Rotterdam, Hong Kong). Regionally situated vendors can then be directed to deliver purchased goods to that entities warehouse.

The consolidator examines and assures the right quantity and, within reason, quality, have been delivered. The importer can release goods for export and importation as needed. That might be to meet a particular production schedule or promotion. The consolidation point may perform other duties as well. Labeling or ticketing services may be "outsourced" if the consolidation point is a lower labor cost location. We did this very successfully for a major cosmetics company with facilities and vendors in Asia and Europe and manufacturing sites in North America.

Outbound Consolidation

The opposite technique will work when the cost of making small export shipments can be reduced by consolidating them into larger consignments and shipping to a "breakbulk" de-consolidator, who then arranges for onward transportation and even the "final kilometer" delivery to the customer. What matters is that in the process of reducing your cost of transportation, you do not violate your service commitment to your customer. Holding orders for consolidation is a great idea as long as you keep the customer.

Duty Reduction Strategies

One of the reasons to buy foreign goods is that they cost less. Offsetting the cost of the good itself are the costs of transportation and duty. Duty reduction techniques are often the consequence of governmental desire to encourage domestic manufacturing and/or increase trade within economic zones.

The starting point in this analysis is determining what the rate of duty is for the commodity to be imported *(see the sections on classification and duty)*. Using *HS* as the starting point, you find the applicable rate of duty in the country's tariff, making note of the existence of preference programs if there are any. Preference programs provide reduced rates for imports of select commodities, usually from less developed countries. An example is GSP, "the generalized system of preferences."

It is important for commodities that may be perceived as dangerous (competitively) to domestic manufacturing to determine whether a quota (a limit on the total number of units) exists. Commodities such as garments, textiles, steel, and others may be subject to quota or countervailing duties that raise a landed cost as a means of protecting domestic industry. Countervailing duty seeks to raise the landed cost of the foreign produced article to obviate subsidies.

If you are only importing for domestic consumption and duty is a significant cost issue, you may wish to consider sourcing from within an economic bloc or country with which a trade agreement exists. For example if are in Mexico and can buy a raw material from Canada or China, the existence of the North American Trade Agreement (NAFTA) will make it cheaper to source from Canada even if the Chinese material is otherwise cheaper.

There are many trade agreements, literally hundreds. It is important to research which might apply to your business in order to lower your landed costs to the lowest possible.

A word of caution is in order. To qualify for duty relief from most trade agreements, the conditions specified must be met. These are often very complex and the penalties for inappropriately claiming the preference can be severe.

If you are planning to use some or all of the import in additional manufacturing, there is a variety of possible strategies that emerge. The technique to use to reduce costs will depend on what will happen to the imported good.

1. Importing a good for resale in the domestic market

2. Importing a raw material for further manufacturing and domestic sale

3. Importing a raw material for further manufacturing and export

4. Importing for manufacturing with some export and domestic sale

5. Importing a material for inventory and re-export

We already addressed trade agreements and programs that apply to specially designated developing countries. The North American Trade Agreement (NAFTA) between Canada, Mexico, and the United States is an example of trade agreement that provides duty relief according to strict rules. The Transpacific Trade Partnership is an agreement currently being negotiated.

Another question that the SME may ask is <u>what form to import</u> the commodity or raw material. This has to do with how far along the line a commodity has gone before reaching its final form. For example, an almond may be raw in bags or it may be crushed and part of a packaged cereal. A battery may be a 12V battery or it may be installed in an automobile. An active pharmaceutical ingredient may be an API or it may be a tablet in a blister pack.

The form of the commodity will impact the commodity classification and the applicable duty. In general, lower rates of duty for manufacturing inputs encourage local manufacturing. It may be preferable to import a commodity in a semi-finished form into a trade bloc and finish the manufacturing there to reduce the cost of duty.

This kind of analysis is worthwhile if your estimated calculations indicate that your business will incur substantial duty, especially if the duty burden will be decisive. It might be beneficial to import semi-finished goods to reduce duty cost. Importing a commodity subject to a high rate of duty and *transforming* it through a manufacturing process is one way that might achieve a cost improvement goal.

In a transformation scenario, the substance must take on a new character in the process. In this way it may be possible to delay the payment of duty. This might be a good cash flow strategy where high rates of duty and value are involved.

If you are going to further manufacture or re-export, either in whole or in part, dutiable goods can be brought into a *customs bonded warehouse* or *free trade zone* or sub-zone and held until used in manufacture and then imported. Duty is paid when the merchandise leaves the duty-free area. Please note that bonded facilities and free trade zones are authorized by the local government and are subject to strict regulations that typically require very careful record-keeping.

Another strategy that is available in most countries is the concept of inward processing, also known as duty drawback. If you are importing a dutiable good for further manufacturing and will subsequently export merchandise containing duty-paid material, you are generally able to recover the duty paid on the import. You need not be the importer yourself to claim drawback. It is possible to negotiate the transfer of rights to drawback from the actual importer.

Drawback is a useful tool if you are using dutiable raw materials in merchandise that will subsequently be sold for export, especially to multiple markets. As in the case of bonded facilities, inward processing requires careful record-keeping. In some countries, including in the United States, customs approval is needed to claim drawback.

Growing The Company Summary

Managing the supply chain as the company evolves is a complex process with many pathways the SME can profit from by understanding the options and choosing the course that will minimize costs while enhancing service to customers. In global networks this is often achieved by integrating systems, sources, and suppliers and making use, wherever it makes sense, of governmental programs that seek to encourage domestic business operations. Deciding the best course is often a balance of personality issues, inexact estimates of cost and projections of benefit realistically obtainable from one course or another.

Part VI - Cross Border Problems Survey

When I conducted the International Chamber of Commerce Survey, I left an open-ended question on what kinds of border barriers traders had actually encountered. Fifty of those responses are listed below for the reader to gain insights. What is notable about these and why I included them is that I reproduce some of them in this book to demonstrate the randomness and unpredictability of bumps along the road. I present them to show how bumps are very much localized to specific ports and even to specific bureaucrats at the specific ports.

The Bumps (problems) in Their Own Words

- An exporter said: On export of 2 containers to Turkey, the container numbers got mixed up on the Vet-certificate attachment. Even though both containers were on the same certificate and invoice, the delay of 10 days cost our customer 800 USD but was paid by us.

- An exporter-importer said: For our company, it is road transportation of goods over Neum corridor (Bosna and Hercegovina). Although delivery of goods is inside EU, passing over Neum results in additional border formality and costs. This applies to all bossiness in Croatia, which is situated south of Neum corridor (Dubrovnik city and nearby islands). We are looking forward to bridging which building was stopped by the government.

- An exporter-importer said: goods held INCORRECTLY claiming in-adherence to SWPB ISPM15 [a wood inspection certificate]; then released after 2 weeks with thousands of dollars of storage costs

- An exporter-importer said: [Customs Duty was paid] on Goods sent for Exhibition to Saudi Arabia for sending and receiving as well in spite of [the goods] being for Exhibition Goods and our office being located in Free Zone.on Goods sent for Exhibition to Saudi Arabia for sending and receiving as well in spite of [the goods] being for Exhibition Goods and our office being located in Free Zone.

- An exporter said: [the] Green Fence Policy from Chinese government that [started] beginning of 2013; [caused] huge delays in ports and high demurrage/detention costs (up to some months).

- An exporter-importer said: I have a case for export into KSA (Kingdom of Saudi Arabia)—here the shipment requires a Certificate of conformity—goods [had been] ready [for] 2 weeks—inspection was done yesterday—now we need the agency to issue the certificate—they need another 1 to 2 weeks—so we lost 4 weeks for just one document.

- An importer said: I just paid a penalty to the shipping company because the Health Authority asked for supplementary analysis and the container was blocked until the result arrived (the analysis arrived after 4 days). Another 3 days was lost for handling from the port to the Health Authority and back to port for custom clearance.

- An importer said: Istanbul Turkey. It is so close, we can both import and export goods. It is the same distance from here as Athens, but customs procedures (TIR vehicle etc) make difficult. For example, I needed an extra part that cost 110 Euros in Turkey. I paid another 80 Euros in transportation (a package of 12 Kg, minimum charge 80 Euros) another 100 Euros for the custom responsible to make the custom clearance plus all the taxes. It takes 10 days to get anything (or send anything) to Turkey. [...] in continuous trade, there are needs of smaller urgent needs.

- An importer-exporter said: Manual documentation processes at point of export from the US to Ecuador resulted in a paperwork omission. The Latin-American customs authority assumed attempted smuggling and held 5 ocean containers for over 10 months. Massive storage charges accrued because of clerical error, which the foreign customs authority assumed was a criminal act.

- An importer said: our company has operated [a] trading business in Bremen for over 20 years. During this time, we [have] faced always unnecessary inspections and examinations without clear reason each year and caused a long delay and much more cost. A [recent] container from COSCO will be extra controlled on [date provided]. It [resulting] in at least a 5-day delay and 400 Euros.

- An exporter-importer said: a packaging material [shipment] held on the border due to malfunction of customs software caused serious delays in production.

- An exporter said: Phytosanitary Treatment of Wood in Germany is much more expensive than in other European countries because the authorities prescribe other chemicals.

- An exporter-importer said: Recently, a shipment of Black Friday/holiday items were pulled for a VACIS exam. It took CBP 5 days to get it to the exam station and then 5 days to inspect. What was getting looked at? We had all the paper work. The items were for children, we had the GCCs. Since the exam delayed the ETA, we had to open our DC so we could get the inventory out to our stores, which was an unexpected additional cost. [A VACIS exam is a US Customs X-Ray of a container looking for contraband].

- An importer said: Regular customs checks of containers in Rotterdam cost demurrage to be paid to the carrier. These cannot be reimbursed [recovered].

- An importer-exporter said: Simple export declarations costing from 40 to 120 Euros [Greece]. Same declarations are performed with no cost by courier companies in UK.

- An importer-exporter said: Speed money to be paid in India.

- An importer-exporter said: The border patrol put a seal on a truck delivering our products from Italy for no reason, and we had to wait on a Sunday for 2 hours to come to take off the seal.

- An importer-exporter said: Turkey—import by customer was delayed due to obscure regulation for more than a week. Case could only be solved by offering money.

- An importer-exporter said: We buy Wire rods from Abu Dhabi (…) and last month, Jebel Ali customs [stopped] caught the truck because of wrong entry papers. They have not cleared it within a week and it was big loss for us.

- An importer said: we expected a container from China at the beginning of December. This container was picked out for a physical control. Now the custom officers found a higher gas concentration (caused by new wheels for wheelbarrows....). So there has to be done ventilation, transportation to a warehouse outside the harbor terminal. Finally, we had to pay 2500 EUR for additional transportation, inspection, ventilation, and we had a delay of 4 weeks to finally receive the container. To avoid this, we decided to do the custom declaration near our hometown in the future and abandon the fiscal clearance.

- An importer-exporter said: We send chemicals, which have to be cooled. Sometimes, we need dry ice for the cooling. Therefore, the transport time has to be fast. Because of delays in USA (financial shutdown), we have to destroy many deliveries.

- An exporter said: We were sending the goods to Russia for exhibition. Goods were passing through Ukraine. Ukrainian customs does not let the goods pass, we had large stand in Russian exhibition with no goods on it.

- An LSP said: When certain specified equipment for a specific capability was specifically duty exempted in order to encourage investment in the sector, the delay in allowing the exemption caused the occurrence of not only demurrage at the port but also container detention charges from the shipping company[y] although the delay was not due to the consignee but because of the Customs, which provided a delay detention refund note to the shipping companies and dockside terminals [which] was not honored by them.

- An association said: Excessive delays at the vehicle and pedestrian frontier into/out of Gibraltar [from Spain] since August 2013 has led to employees to being late for work, meetings missed, and decisions delayed. This costs Gibraltar's businesses money.

- An importer-exporter said: 2-month blocked export in France due to HS-Code and Dual Use Classification review.

- An importer-exporter said: [The] Brazil-Import License System leads to shipping delays and loss of turnover.

- A service provider said: Different IT systems for customs communication in each EU Member State [are an issue]. As a service provider for ASP-[passport] services, [we have] no direct customs communication with, e.g., Spain or Italy without local VAT—not possible in this case for ICS; we have to use a Spanish partner to send the messages for our clients.

- An importer said: As we are in "seasonal business," any non-calculable variation in import-processes [i.e., unpredictability] is directly affecting on-time shelf availability of products, respectively, sell through at non-discounted prices. Further to that, retail-partners hold us liable for delays. Very early importation creates stock risks.

- An exporter said: Greece and other countries with expanded island characteristics. Islands should have the facilities for arranging customs clearance on the spot. In our case (Kythera Greece), goods need to travel to Piraeus (Athens —mainland), then to the customs for clearance and then to the transport company or port for export. This is adding a great cost in the whole procedure and takes up more time as well.

- An importer-exporter said: Being air conditioner manufacturers, we could not deliver window units within the peak months due to border delays and the orders ultimately had to be cancelled and we had to return the LC. Border delays at Kingdom of Saudi Arabia sited.

- An exporter-importer said: Border delays in Kingdom of Saudi Arabia affects the business as we cannot meet the customer deadlines for delivery. The certification procedures for KSA & Kuwait even make more delays.

- An importer-exporter said: Brazil [has the] highest import delays, Russia [has the highest] legal uncertainty and India—[is] very protective. The complexity of non-customs-related legislation [regulations] especially in agriculture /veterinary and environmentally driven issues

- An importer-exporter said: Brazil—inconsistent application of regulations leads to lengthy border delays, affecting both distribution and manufacturing. Inconsistent application of rules/regulations. Difference in regulations for import/export vs other agencies, for example tax authority.

- An importer-exporter said: China's last-minute imposition of cargo holds on Canadian pork shipments owing to long, very minor establishment discrepancies in CIQ's data base...."ST. instead of Street" on Official Meat Inspection Certificates as reason to hold shipments.....needless excessive exams by FDA on imported processed vegetables a couple dozen shipments held and many inspected and sent to lab for analysis with all product being found perfectly fine and released.

- An importer-exporter said: Chinese Customs [do] have different classification positions [interpretations].

- An exporter said: Poor communication/language (English) skills [clearing] at port in China.

- An importer-exporter said: Clearing paper reels though customs in Santos, Brazil, warehouse. Different Interpretation of INCO terms than in Europe.

- An importer-exporter said: Company is exporter of clay roof tiles in Bosnia and Herzegovina but we need to provide customs office documents ([for]their approval) for export simplified procedure—for each border crossing. Entering (Croatia) EU, we need to declare each truck with safety or annunciation declaration for each truck and wait for customs code for export and (regarding that we have weekly customs clearance[s]) our forward[ing] agent need[s] to declare again customs clearance.

- An importer-exporter said: Custom office refused to accept value on the invoice (pleasure boat) even it was issued directly by the factory and even though we are official distributor and importer for that factory and their product. The boat was blocked as we could not get import documents, they charge[d] us for much higher value and VAT rate than it was on the invoice.

- An importer-exporter said: Demurrage of Containers to Qatar due to delays in legalization at the embassy.

- An importer-exporter said: In India, importer should submit the original copy of certificate of origin for preferential duty treatment. When it comes to shipment via airplane, cargoes come before arrival of document about 2~3 days, but without CoO, importers do not have an option to get duty reduction, as duty refund procedure takes more than a year. [Also, Inconsistent practice over same law/regulations between local customs. India/China/Russia].

- An exporter said: In several cases (especially Brazil and India), the foreign customs demanded certificates or a kind of letter according to their local law, which we did not know and are; therefore, difficult to provide and understand.

- An importer-exporter said: Most of our issues are not related to Customs in the US specifically. They are OGA related, specifically FDA. FDA consistently pulls *product and holds it without exam at our expense. We cannot deliver it because our facilities tend to be more than 50 miles from the nearest district office.*

- An exporter said: Our main activity is apparel CMT (cut, make &trimmings). We received several times fabrics directly from non-EU suppliers that were bought by our EU customers and sent directly to Romania. Customs must be made directly by the EU customer in this case, but always this is long (they have to be able to pay directly the import tax and 24% VAT to Romania fiscal authorities). We are losing precious production time due to this. It will be useful if we could claim back the tax and VAT paid by us for our customers. If we pay them now, they cannot be claimed back because we have to provide to the authorities that we paid the invoice as well (which is not the case, because the goods do not belong to us).

- An importer-exporter said: see the Uzbekistan example in #4 above. Unable to fulfill contractual delivery commitment to customer due to inability to get the required stamp from the EU, where wet stamps are no longer used and are in violation of EU rules.

- An Importer-Exporter said: Slow handling, unclear internal communication and flow of information between German export control authority BAFA and Customs, causing delays, unnecessary bureaucracy and paper work, frustrating customers and blocking business.

- An Importer-Exporter said: Slow import procedure in China, delay lead to perishables getting spoilt; Chinese import authorities demanding unnecessary documents according to international agreements; US authorities imposing new regulations on short notice; US authorities imposing ban on certain plants although grown in sterile tissue culture, which cannot be infested by any pests. [Added]—Use of reference pricing. Restrictive procedural processes, such as requiring a wet stamp on the shipping country's export documents even when the exporting country's processes are 100% electronic and wet stamps no longer exist (i.e., Uzbekistan).

- An exporter said: Unnecessary licenses (e.g., CEMT) are requested for non-Greek trucks by the Greek customs for export to non EU countries when goods are moved within the limits of EU. (non-compliance to EU laws) This increases the

cost of transport and final product price and to complicated logistics, leading to losing customers.

- An importer-exporter said: We are importing regularly reagents which "can" contain animal content. Inspection at the border has to be done for 100% although we have only 3-5%, which needs to be controlled. As AEO-F, we have the simplified procedures but for these products, it is not allowed and we have to use the normal procedure, which slows down our end-to-end process dramatically. No chance to get a simplification here for the reagents without animal content.

- An LSP said: With new agricultural clearance system in Mexico, release times may take up to 24 hours, delaying the timely delivery of goods as scheduled in factories.

While the foregoing may suggest a world of chaos, and to some extent it is, you can take some solace in the knowledge that millions and millions of shipments are made every year and most make it, payment and all. So, are there steps an SME can take to avoid these bumps? These are some. For example, in the case of the notorious FDA compliance bureaucrat at New York's Kennedy Airport, some importers simply brought goods into alternative nearby ports. Foreknowledge of potential bumps can be somewhat effective in avoiding them. What are some strategies to avoid problems as much as possible?

1. Work with logistics service providers familiar with your markets and industry. Ask for references in similar businesses and markets. Call and ask what problems they have encountered. It is refreshing that so many businesses are willing to share experiences.

2. Listen to your customers/suppliers. Learn what their experience has been and what can be done to avoid them. For example, for a long time, Brazil required signatures in black ink. Knowing that will prevent the daunting blue ink fiasco.

3. Assure that your documents are clean, crisp, and understandable and contain the required information. As a forwarder, I recall an auto parts supplier whose invoices went on for 30 or 40 pages. That document always caused issues. What is actually needed:

a. The words "Commercial Invoice".

b. Date of the invoice (sometimes, the bill of lading date).

c. Names (seller, buyer).

d. References (purchase order numbers, invoice number).

e. Ports of exit and entry.

f. Description of the goods (best to use the HS description as a header followed by the trade name). If you have 800 parts to list, prepare a pro-forma invoice for customs purposes so the officer doesn't need to wade through pages of meaningless data). In communications with the customer (or if you are the customer), it would be good to clarify whether the HS number itself should be printed on the invoice. I say this because there have been national disagreements on the HS number to be used. So clarify this before doing it.

g. Price per unit and total invoice amount and currency.

h. Directly beside the invoice total, state the prevailing Incoterm (EXW, CIF) with a named place (e.g., CIF Liverpool). If you are prepaying and adding expenses, list them separately with an amount. FAS Hong Kong $12,000 USD, Ocean freight 1,000, Insurance 500, CIF Miami $13,500 US

i. If you have a letter of credit, print the LC references on the invoice along with the verbiage in the LC (the goods description).

j. If your customer has provided special clauses to print on the invoice, do so (e.g., Contains No Red #3).

k. Certify the invoice with words like "Certified True &Correct" and sign the document in black ink.

l. If the customer needs five signed invoices, send seven or eight.

4. For exports, have your forwarder email your customer shipping details as soon as known and request confirmation of receipt of the communication and the goods. Create a follow-up system so you know, positively, that the goods have arrived. Same for imports. In other words, do not wait for a delay to become a disaster.

5. If you are working with a challenging market (e.g., Russia, Iran) be sure that you are working with Logistic Service Provider, Tax, Customs, with specific expert knowledge of the market.

Appendix A - INCOTERMS

I have referred to INCOTERMS in this primer, this appendix is a brief bit on what they are and why they matter.

As indicated at several points in the book, it is important that you and your business partners, namely your customers and suppliers, have the same understanding of who is undertaking what responsibility and who is paying for what.

A ship laden with 4,000 containers hits a particularly severe North Atlantic winter storm. Thirty-foot waves slam the ship, causing 15% rolls, lashing holding containers on the deck snap, sending 70 containers into the sea. Three of those are yours. But you have not paid for them and your terms with your Pakistani supplier are 90 days net. Well, if you do not receive the goods, are you compelled to pay for them? The question, is who was responsible for insuring the goods against a loss such as this. The answer is found in the INCOTERM used in the contract. Courts, civil authorities, banks, carriers—all the players in global trade agree to what the terms mean and enforce the provisions.

A detailed discussion of the INCOTERMS is beyond this book, but there are plenty of reference works you can turn to for details, the promulgator of the terms themselves, the International Chamber of Commerce. Use the link below to access the ICC and information about the terms. What I have done below is a very simplified version that you can use to assure you and your business partner that you are aligned on what you meant when you quoted your selling prices.

EXW – EX WORKS (… named place such as "Cleveland") The Seller's only responsibility is to make the goods available at the Seller's premises. The Buyer bears full costs and risks of moving the goods from there to destination.

FCA – FREE CARRIER (… named place…") The Seller delivers the goods, cleared for export, to the carrier selected by the Buyer. The Seller loads the goods if the carrier pickup is at the Seller's premises. From that point, the Buyer bears the costs and risks of moving the goods to destination.

CPT – CARRIAGE PAID TO (…destination such as "Antwerp") The Seller pays for moving the goods to destination. From the time the goods are transferred to the first carrier, the Buyer bears the risks of loss or damage.

CIP – CARRIAGE AND INSURANCE PAID TO (… named place of destination such as Los Angeles) The Seller pays for moving the goods to destination. From the time the goods are transferred to the first carrier, the Buyer bears the risks of loss or damage. The Seller, however, purchases the cargo insurance.

DAT – DELIVERED AT TERMINAL (… named terminal at port or place of destination) The Seller delivers when the goods, once unloaded from the arriving means of transport, are placed at the Buyer's disposal at a named terminal at the named port or place of destination. "Terminal" includes any place, whether covered or not, such as a quay, warehouse, container yard or road, rail or air cargo terminal. The Seller bears all risks involved in bringing the goods to and unloading them at the terminal at the named port or place of destination.

DAP – DELIVERED AT PLACE (… named place of destination) The Seller delivers when the goods are placed at the Buyer's disposal on the arriving means of transport ready for unloading at the named place of destination. The Seller bears all risks involved in bringing the goods to the named place.

DDP – DELIVERED DUTY PAID (… named place such as "Paris") The Seller delivers the goods—cleared for import—to the Buyer at destination. The Seller bears all costs and risks of moving the goods to destination, including the payment of Customs duties and taxes.

MARITIME-ONLY TERMS

FAS – FREE ALONGSIDE SHIP (…such as Hong Kong) The Seller delivers the goods to the origin port. From that point, the Buyer bears all costs and risks of loss or damage.

CFR – COST AND FREIGHT (… named port such as Rotterdam) The Seller clears the goods for export and pays the costs of moving the goods to destination. The Buyer bears all risks of loss or damage.

CIF – COST INSURANCE AND FREIGHT (… named port of destination) The Seller clears the goods for export and pays the costs of moving the goods to the port of destination. The Buyer bears all risks of loss or damage. The Seller, however, purchases the cargo insurance.

You can use the link below to read more about the INCOTERMS or buy a copy.

http://www.iccwbo.org/products-and-services/trade-facilitation/incoterms-2010/

Appendix B - Trade Documentation List

As reference and to further illustrate the potential complexity of international trade the list below is from Hong Kong TDC list of common Import / Export Documents. They suggest that SMEs get familar with preparing them. See more at: http://hong-kong-economy-research.hktdc.com/business-news/article/Small-Business-Resources/Common-Import-Export-Documents/sbr/en/1/1X000000/1X006MLL.htm#sthash.GlZqZEqZ.dpuf

The types of documents involved in international trade are, commercial documents, financial documents, transport documents, insurance documents and other international trade related documents. In processing the export consignment, documentation may be executed in up to four contracts: the export sales contract, the contract of carriage, the contract of finance and the contract of cargo insurance.

Commercial Documents

Quotation - An offer to sell goods stating the price, details of quality, quantity, trade terms, delivery terms and payment terms.

Sales Contract- An agreement between the buyer and the seller stipulating every detail of the transaction. Since this is a legally binding document, it is therefore advisable to seek legal advice before signing the contract.

Pro Forma Invoice - An invoice provided by a supplier prior to the shipment of merchandise, informing the buyer of the kinds and quantities of goods to be sent, their value, and importation specifications (weight, size and similar characteristics). This is not issued for demanding payment but may be used when applying for an import licence / permit or arranging foreign currency or other funding purposes.

Commercial Invoice- A formal demand note for payment issued by the exporter to the importer for goods sold under a sales contract. It should give details of the goods sold, payment terms and trade terms. It is also used for the customs clearance of goods and sometimes for foreign exchange purpose by the importer.

Packing List- A list with detailed packing information of the goods shipped.

Inspection Certificate - A report issued by an independent surveyor (inspection company) or the exporter on the specifications of the shipment, including quality, quantity, and / or price, required by certain buyers and countries.

Insurance Policy - An insurance document, with full details of the insurance coverage, evidencing insurance has been taken out on the goods shipped.

Insurance Certificate - This certifies that the shipment has been insured under a given open policy and is to cover loss of or damage to the cargo while in transit.

Product Testing Certificate - This certifies the products are conformed to a certain international / national technical standard, such as product quality, safety and specifications.

Health Certificate - Document issued by the competent country when agricultural or food products are being exported, to certify that they comply with the relevant legislation in the exporter's country and were in good condition at time of inspection, prior to shipment and fit for human consumption.

Phytosanitary Certificate - Frequently an international requirement that any consignment of plants or planting materials importing into a country shall be accompanied by a Phytosanitary Certificate issued by the exporting country stating that the consignment is found substantially free from diseases and pests and conforms with the current phytosanitary regulations of the importing country. Application of the certificate in Hong Kong should be made to the Agriculture and Fisheries Department.

Fumigation Certificate - A pest control certificate issued to certify that the concerned products have been undergone the quarantine and pre-shipment fumigation by the approved fumigation service providers. It is mainly required by the US, Canada, Australia, New Zealand and UK's customs on solid wood packing material from Hong Kong and the Chinese Mainland.

ATA Carnet - An international customs document used to obtain a duty-free temporary admission for goods such as exhibits for international trade fairs, samples and professional equipment, into the countries that are signatories to the ATA Convention.

Consular Invoice - A document required by some foreign countries, showing shipment information such as consignor, consignee, and value description, etc. Certified by a consular official of the importing country stationed in the foreign country, it is used by the country's customs officials to verify the value, quantity and nature of the shipment.

Transport Documents

Shipping Order S/O - A document with details of the cargo and the shipper's requirements, and is the basic document for preparing other transport documents such as bill of lading, air waybill, etc.

Dock Receipt D/R or Mate's Receipt - A receipt to confirm the receipt of cargo on quay / warehouse pending shipment. The dock receipt is used as documentation to prepare a bill of lading. It has no legal role regarding processing financial settlement.

Bill of Lading (B/L) - An evidence of contract between the shipper of the goods and the carrier. The customer usually needs the original as proof of ownership to take possession of the goods. There are two types: a STRAIGHT bill of lading is non-negotiable and a negotiable or shipper's ORDER bill of lading (also a title document) which can be bought, sold or traded while goods are in transit and is used for many types of financing transactions.

House Bill of Lading (Groupage) - A bill of lading issued by a forwarder and, in many cases, not a title document. Shippers choosing to use a house bill of lading, should clarify with the bank whether it is acceptable for letter of credit purpose before the credit is opened. Advantages include less packing, lower insurance premiums, quicker transit, less risk of damage and lower rates than cargo as an individual parcel / consignment.

Sea Waybill - A receipt for cargo which incorporates the contract of carriage between the shipper and the carrier but is non-negotiable and is therefore not a title document.

Air Waybill (AWB) - A kind of waybill used for the carriage of goods by air. This serves as a receipt of goods for delivery and states the condition of carriage but is not a title document or transferable / negotiable instrument.

House Air Waybill (HAWB) - An air consignment note issued by an air freight agent to provide the cargo description and records. Again, it is not a title document.

Shipping Guarantee - Usually a pre-printed form provided by a shipping company or the bank, given by an importer's bank to the shipping company to replace the original transport document. The consignee may then in advance take delivery of goods against a shipping guarantee without producing the original bill of lading. The consignee and the importer bank will be responsible for any loss or charges occurred to the shipping company if fault is found in the collection. It is usually used with full margin or trust receipt to protect the bank's control to the goods.

Packing List (sometimes as packing note) - A list providing information needed for transportation purpose, such as details of invoice, buyer, consignee, country of origin, vessel / flight date, port / airport of loading, port / airport of discharge, place of delivery, shipping marks / container number, weight / volume of merchandise and the fullest details of the goods, including packing information.

Financial Documents

Documentary Credit D/C - A bank instrument (issuing or opening bank), at the request of the buyer, evidencing the bank's undertaking to the seller to pay a certain sum of money provided that specific requirements set out in the D/C are satisfied.

Standby Credit - An arrangement between a customer and his bank by which the customer may enjoy the convenience of cashing cheques, up to a value. Or a credit set up between the exporter and the importer guaranteeing the exporter will pay the importer a certain amount of money if the contract is not fulfilled. It is also known as performance bond. This is usually found in large transactions, such as crude oil, fertilizers, fishmeal, sugar, urea, etc.

Collection Instruction - An instruction given by an exporter to its banker, which empowers the bank to collect the payment subject to the contract terms on behalf of the exporter.

Bill of Exchange (B/E) or Draft - An unconditional written order, in which the importer addressed to and required by the exporter to pay on demand or at a future date a certain amount of money to the order of a person or bearer.

Trust Receipt (T/R) - A document to release a merchandise by a bank to a buyer (the bank still retains title to the merchandise), the buyer, who obtains the goods for processing is obligated to maintain the goods distinct from the remainder of his / her assets and to hold them ready for repossession by the bank.

Promissory Note - A financial instrument that is negotiable evidencing the obligations of the foreign buyer to pay to the bearer.

Government Documents

Certificate of Origin (CO) - This certifies the place of manufacture of the exported goods to meet the requirements of the importing authorities.

Certificate of Origin Generalized Systems of Preferences (GSP) Form A (or as Form A) - A CO to support the claim for preferential tariff entry (a reduced or zero rate) of the exporting country's products into the GSP donors under the GSP they operate. In general, a Form A is issued only when the goods concerned have met both the origin rules of the preference receiving country as well as the origin criteria of the respective donor country's GSP.

Import / Export Declaration - A statement made to the Director of Customs at port of entry / exit, declaring full particulars of the shipment, eg. the nature and the destination / exporting country of the ship's cargo. Its primary use is for compiling trade statistics.

Import / Export Licence - A document issued by a relevant government department authorising the imports and exports of certain controlled goods.

International Import Certificate (IIC) - A statement issued by the government of country of destination, certifying the imported strategic goods will be disposed of in the designated country. In Hong Kong, it is issued only to meet an exporting country's requirement.

Delivery Verification Certificate (DVC) - A statement issued by the government of country of destination, certifying a specific strategic commodity has been arrived in the designated country. In Hong Kong, it is issued only to meet an exporting country's requirement.

Landing Certificate - A document issued by the government of country of destination, certifying a specific commodity has been arrived in the designated country. In Hong Kong, it is issued by the Census and Statistics Department. Application requirements include letter stating the reason for the application, import declaration & receipt; bill of lading, sea waybill & land manifest; supplier's invoice; and packing list (if any).

Customs Invoice - A document specified by the customs authorities of the importing countries stating the selling price, costs for freight, insurance, packing and payment terms, etc, for the purpose of determining the customs value.

Afterword - Parting Comments

I thought it would be easy to write this book. I have a lot of years of experience and a lot of insights to convey. But it was not easy because there is so much to write about and I wanted to write a little book that people could read without a lot of effort. What turned out is longer than I wanted but too short to tell the whole story. Nevertheless, I am hopeful a key aim has been accomplished and that is to sensitize you to topics than can help grow your global business by recognizing and exploiting logistical opportunities while avoiding dangers you would not otherwise seen coming.

Tony Barone